LAKELAND HIGH TARNS

LAKELAND
HIGH TARNS

JOHN DREWS

David & Charles

FOR MY PARENTS

All photographs by the author

Tarn specifications are based on research by the
Brathay Exploration Group

A DAVID & CHARLES BOOK

A catalogue record for this book is available from the
British Library.

ISBN 0 7153 0334 1

Designed and typeset by Drum and Company
and printed in Italy by Lego SpA
for David & Charles
Brunel House Newton Abbot Devon

*Right: The clouds break on a summer afternoon, spotlighting
Seathwaite Tarn. Viewed from Levers Hawse, looking towards
Dunnerdale*
*p1: At Wise Een Tarn as the summer sun sets behind
Coniston's fells*
*p2: An autumn morning above Nethermost Cove, looking
towards Striding Edge and Red Tarn*

CONTENTS

INTRODUCTION

Winter sunset at Seathwaite Tarn

The most celebrated features of the English Lake District are the peaks and of course the lakes themselves. No effort is required to visit any of them, as they can all be viewed and to a limited extent enjoyed by car.

But the real treasures of the area lie concealed in combes and hollows up among the Lakeland Fells, just waiting to be explored. These are the high tarns – small mountain 'lakes' that occupy the unlikeliest of locations, constantly surprising and always charming.

I knew nothing of them until the fateful day I was invited by a friend to fish, swim and generally disport ourselves in the hills. And so, despite my reservations that we would not get any further than the Grasmere pubs, two middle-aged men found themselves wheezing their way upwards from the valley. It is a day I will never forget. Resplendent in our hob-nailed boots and encumbered by suitcases, bulky sleeping bags and umpteen other items that one should never carry, we made our way to one of the most accessible of the mountain gems, Easedale Tarn.

I didn't know what to expect, but the cold crystal stream complete with waterfalls and pools which refreshed us on our way up also served to heighten my enthusiasm for the adventure. The fact that there were other people there when we reached our goal didn't diminish my sense of discovery one jot. I was struck by the sense of wonder amongst those who had taken the trouble to get there, to escape the excesses of the commercialised Lakeland areas.

Later, after our halcyon day of angling and bathing, we made camp by the water's edge, beneath a spectacular canopy of stars. Since that time, although I have often been away from them, I have never really left the tarns.

As a general rule the high tarns are of two types. First, there are the combe or corrie rock basin tarns located at the valley heads, close to the peak summits. These were created by the tremendous rotational, gouging effect of glaciers thousands of years ago. Then there are the meltwater tarns found on lower ridges or 'hanging valleys'. These are held in place by terminal moraine – rock and debris scraped out of the mountainsides and then deposited by the retreating glaciers at the end of each ice age. The ice cap was so vast that some Lakeland rocks have been found as far south as Cheshire.

This book contains only a few of the many tarns in the Lake District. With just two exceptions, those that I have chosen are accessible only on foot and lend themselves to circular routes through some of Lakeland's most impressive scenery. Each walk is entirely distinctive, with no repetition, either of tarns or of route sections. Nor is there any need for significant backtracking; none of the routes require one to retrace one's steps.

There is considerable variation in both the distance and the difficulty of these walks, but each belongs to one of three categories: short routes of no more than three hours' duration, medium routes of three to four hours and long routes of four to six hours. The majority fall into the short and medium categories. Of course they can all be spread over a whole day or even an entire weekend if you want to take advantage of the camping and fishing opportunities.

Some routes can be tackled by complete beginners without any difficulty; indeed, it is even possible to have an enjoyable day simply visiting some of the starting locations. Other routes will satisfy the most experienced walkers.

The number of tarns per walk ranges from one to three, and all have been photographed, together with other features of interest such as waterfalls, special views and lakes. This is the first time that a walking guide has targeted the tarns, and the first photographic work to concentrate on them. My reason for writing it is quite simple – it needed to be done. Too many books have overlooked these magical places, causing countless walkers to miss their soothing qualities. Here one can truly relax and enjoy the high country.

Apart from maps, there is a brief summary of each route which gives an at-a-glance guide to the start/finish point, the number of the relevant Ordnance Survey map, the distance and the time it is likely to take. The summaries are colour coded for quick reference: short route, medium route, long route. These times are purely personal estimates of how long it would take a reasonably fit person to complete the walk *excluding* breaks, and assuming that only a light pack is carried. A description of any special needs such as fishing permits is also included in the summaries. Where no mention of such permits is made, only the standard National Rivers Authority licence is required.

Always carry a map and compass. If you should lose your way, it is important to remember that this happens to everybody at some time, and not to be unduly disturbed. In such a situation trust your map and compass *not your instincts*, as appearances on the fells are often deceptive. Take this book with you, or at least copies of the maps. You will find them very helpful where paths fork and cut across your way. Many of these paths are unmapped by the Ordnance Survey, but I include the major ones. Please note that the description of a route does not necessarily signify a right of way. It is only with the landowners' consent and understanding that many of the most popular paths remain open. If people stray from the paths, climb walls or leave gates open, it could lead to the loss of public access.

The weather can change dramatically within minutes, so pack a lightweight waterproof suit. Waterproof footwear is also advisable as there are patches of marsh on some of these walks. The Lake District weatherline can be consulted before venturing out; forecasts are available on 01768 775757.

I hope the sun shines brightly on your walk, allowing you to experience the thrill of these swimming pools in the sky. Perhaps you will be fortunate enough to witness a multi-hued dawn or sunset faithfully reflected by one of these glittering mountain jewels.

CHAPTER 1

HAWESWATER AND MARDALE

Late afternoon sunshine highlights the Haweswater Hotel in its autumn finery. Viewed looking north from the hotel garden

Those fortunate enough to have seen it in its unspoilt state say that Mardale was once the most rustic and isolated valley in Lakeland. It was graced by the lake known as Haweswater, but at an altitude of 694ft (212m) this was the highest lake in England and therefore presented far too tempting a proposition for use as a reservoir to be left in peace forever.

And so, just before World War II, Haweswater was dammed at its northern outflow by Manchester Corporation to boost the water supply for their city, 75 miles (120km) distant. This resulted in the water level rising by 100ft (30m) at times of high catchment, trebled the lake's surface area and extended its length from 2½ miles to a little under 4 miles (6km). Also it necessitated the evacuation and subsequent drowning of the idyllic hamlet of Mardale Green, nestled at the far end of the valley beneath the wooded Rigg and the mountains.

Nowadays, during the summer months, the water sometimes recedes far enough to reveal the hamlet ruins and produces a white band of bare rock that surrounds the shore. The buildings have been reduced to rubble, but the walls of tracks and fields have for the most part survived, along with the stone bridge. Although the original site can just be discerned, the church was demolished before the flooding, its windows and some of the stone incorporated into the reservoir draw-off tower in an attempt to soften its image.

For many people there is an eerie attraction about ghost villages. In 1984, after the worst drought for 100 years, the ruins were visited by such overwhelming numbers that the local police had to block off the valley. The old road to Mardale was on the western shore, but modern visitors gain access by means of the present one on the opposite side that terminates in a small car park adjacent to the site of the doomed hamlet.

This is the starting point for two walks that include all the finest features and places of interest in this stunning area. Lovers of wildlife will find it particularly enjoyable, as the only eagles in the country are to be found here. There is also a peregrine falcons' nest surprisingly close to the road at the northern end of the lake. There have been a number of unconfirmed sightings of very rare pine martens in the vicinity, while badgers and foxes are much more common.

BLEA WATER AND HIGH STREET

This walk of around four hours' duration visits the deepest tarn, the highest Roman road and the only eagles in England.

From Mardale, the path rises gradually alongside Blea Water Beck and almost immediately the impression of rugged wilderness starts to dominate one's senses, with the high ground of Harter Fell, Mardale Ill Bell and Rough Crag beckoning the walker onward and higher. The ears are filled with the sound of waterfalls in the beck as it cascades down in full view, and across the valley head Small Water's outflow stream rushes down to join it.

The way up to Blea Water takes the form of two distinct steps separated by the marshland known as Mardale Waters. From here Harter Fell is even more impressive, seeming to have grown in stature as our path moved away from it. Up ahead, the high back wall of Blea Water's combe looms ever larger, and then the tarn itself appears.

Blea Water is the king of the Lakeland tarns and something of a geological enigma. With a maximum depth of 207ft (63m), it is by far the deepest, and this depth can only be beaten by Wastwater and Windermere among the lakes themselves. It is located at an altitude of 1,584ft (482m) in a rocky combe formed by the peaks of High Street and Riggindale Crag. The depth and shape of the combe have led many in the past to believe that the tarn marked the site of an extinct volcano, and some of the locals still refer to it as such. More recent investigations, however, discredit this theory and reveal that

Eagle country. Riggindale, Kidsty Pike and Haweswater viewed from above Rowantreethwaite Beck

there were a series of freeze and thaw periods that permeated the rock basin, with the rotational and scooping effect of successive glaciers biting ever deeper into what is now the tarn bed. However, why this should happen here with such marked effect and not in other places is still debatable, and it has been designated as a Site of Special Scientific Interest.

At least four tarns in the district are named Blea. The name comes from a word that can mean blue, dark or cold. The clear water here has a green tint, but for the most part is darkened by the high surrounding mountains. This effect creates a lonely, mysterious aura and welcome shade for the native brown trout.

The only sound here comes from an inlet stream as it crashes down almost vertically from High Street. A large tarn, it is circular in shape with a diameter of around 360yd (330m). It is said that the massive body of water can be rocked in this basin when a strong wind blows from over the towering back face of the combe – by all accounts a truly awesome spectacle. The steep surrounding walls present a problem for those wishing to camp here, as they make it very difficult to pitch a tent comfortably near the shore. In any case, the landowners do not encourage camping in this environmentally important area.

Next on offer is a view of wild and remote Riggindale from Caspel Gate. Riggindale occupies such an isolated position that it remains a sanctuary and grazing ground for wild deer that stray over from their more regular area to the north, where the Martindale red deer herd is over 600 strong.

Some way beneath Caspel Gate and to the right, hidden on the rocky incline of Rough Crag, lies a retreat of another kind: Hugh's Cave, named after one Hugh Holme who was involved in the Canterbury Conspiracy against King John in 1208. When the plot was uncovered, he fled north and by chance came into Mardale, taking refuge in the cave where he stayed until after John's death. He remained an outlaw and declared himself the King of Mardale, passing on his 'crown' to subsequent generations until the last of the male line died in 1885. The family endeared themselves to the local population to such an extent that at the final service given at Mardale church in 1935, the Bishop of Carlisle offered prayers for all the living descendants.

Moving on, a real sense of altitude now begins to build as the path picks its way through the rocky ground heading up towards Long Stile. A look backwards here shows Rough Crag presenting an impressive picture as its upper heights bisect the valley of Riggindale and the depression of Mardale Waters. After the ascent of Long Stile, a wide and far reaching view of the mountains opens up ahead on the approach to the Roman road High Street, after which this fell is named. The tarn-cum-reservoir of Hayeswater (not to be confused with Haweswater) can be seen in the valley below.

High Street is the highest Roman road in England, and is still used as a footpath. Linking the forts of Galava (now Ambleside) and Brovacum near Penrith, its 25 miles (40km) must have provided a good day's march for the legions as they laboured under loads of stone. It is assumed that this road and others like it were built at such an elevation to provide a degree of protection from the still-untamed natives who populated the lower slopes. At that time the slopes would still have been densely forested, affording many opportunities for ambush.

High Street's plateau is so flat and open that the locals used to hold annual festivals here, hauling monumental amounts of food and drink up to it to fuel their enjoyment of sporting activities such as wrestling and horse racing. Some evidence of the insobriety at these meetings can be found in the well-known legend of a local fox hunter who spotted a fox running along the hilltop. He gave chase at full pelt until he disappeared over the cliff, falling in an ungraceful arc

Left: Blea Water's awesome combe, viewed from High Street on an early summer morning. Artlecrag Pike and Harter Fell form the background

almost 800ft (240m) onto rocks. Incredibly, some accounts relate that he managed to get to his feet and called upon the horrified onlookers to continue the pursuit before he collapsed, stone dead. Others state that he suffered bruises and lacerations to his skull, but survived to tell the tale. Later, possibly because of this accident, the festivities were transferred to the Dun Bull Inn down at Mardale Green.

The wide and stony track of High Street descends gently towards the Straits of Riggindale, when suddenly the full length of Riggindale is revealed below, a breathtaking view.

The unmistakable summit of Kidsty Pike 2,559ft (780m) is the next destination, descending to Kidsty Howes. On the ridge to our left, overlooking the lake, lie the ruins of the ancient British fort on Castle Crag. During the Middle Ages this site was again used to defend the region, when a large Scottish raiding party was cut down by local archers.

The path now lies on the opposite side of Riggindale from where Caspel Gate and Long Stile were scaled. There is an uninterrupted view across the valley directly to Hugh's Cave and then along the ridge to Eagle Crag. Eagles abounded in the Lake District at one time but they were hunted to extinction by farmers and sportsmen. The last one is believed to have been shot near Tarn at Leaves about 170 years ago. It is a glowing tribute to the splendours of Riggindale that in 1969 the eagles chose to reappear here, of all places in England.

At the time of writing (spring 1994), a total of fifteen chicks have been successfully reared, aided in no small part by volunteers from the Royal Society for the Protection of Birds. These dedicated people have kept a round-the-clock vigil since the birds' reappearance.

They operate a hide in the valley basin which is open to the public every day from 1 March through to 31 August. As hosts they are both knowledgeable and extremely helpful. Telescopes are provided free, and the volunteers will direct them for anyone to see exactly where the eagles are at any given moment. Visibility is best in the mornings, with the sun to the rear of the hide.

A friend of mine was informed that the current birds are not the original pair, as three males and two females are known to have used the site. When I asked how this could happen, one of the volunteers casually replied that it is a simple matter for such a bird, on finding itself alone, to soar to a height of 4,000ft (1,200m) from where it can be seen by other eagles in southern Scotland!

On leaving the hide you will come across an especially peaceful area where the sparsely wooded promontory of Speaking Crag reaches out into Haweswater. When the water level is high it is hard to believe that this area has been altered by human interference, as it retains such a serene air, still and silent.

A condition of planning permission for the flooding of the valley was that a replacement for the Dun Bull Inn and a new road should be constructed. The original plan was to build a hotel by the Rigg, the densely wooded area which the path now follows. But for reasons which are now obscure, it was eventually placed on the opposite shore. It is open all day throughout the year with non-residents welcome. As you enjoy some well-earned refreshment on the terrace overlooking the lake, remember cavernous and brooding depths, crystal streams and towering heights. Think of marching legions, soaring eagles and know that one day you'll be back.

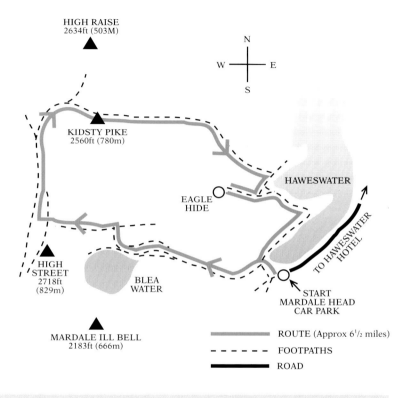

HIGH RAISE
2634ft (503M)

KIDSTY PIKE
2560ft (780m)

HAWESWATER

EAGLE
HIDE

HIGH
STREET
2718ft
(829m)

BLEA
WATER

TO HAWESWATER
HOTEL

START
MARDALE HEAD
CAR PARK

MARDALE ILL BELL
2183ft (666m)

ROUTE (Approx 6½ miles)

FOOTPATHS

ROAD

ROUTE SUMMARY

MAP: OS Outdoor Leisure Map 5

START: Mardale Head car park, Haweswater, GR 469107

DISTANCE: Approximately 6½ miles (10.5km)

TIME: 3½ – 4 hours

DIFFICULTY: High level route

ROUTE DIRECTIONS

The only approach to Haweswater for motorists is from the north via Askham or from the east via Shap. These are the last places where provisions for the walk and for camping can be bought. Any other items such as fishing tackle or outdoor equipment are available from Penrith, the nearest major town. Parking space is limited at Mardale, so try to arrive early.

1 At the carpark gate, there is a metal sign denoting the three paths of Gatescarth Pass, Nan Bield Pass and the bridleway to Bampton. Go through the gate here, immediately crossing the beck. The path rises gently next to a dry stone wall on your right.

2 After about 30yd (25m), the wall turns sharply right, with a path alongside sign-posted 'Public Footpath Bampton'. It crosses two footbridges. After the second (and major one), turn left at the path T-junction.

3 This path to Blea Water goes up two distinct sections or steps alongside Blea Water Beck. Approaching the top of the first step, where the highest waterfall of this section flows out from Mardale Waters, there is a tiny cairn on the right of the main path. This marks the beginning of a very faint path that turns right and up the hillside. If you manage to locate this path, take it – it will avoid possible confusion later as the main path peters out in places. If, however, you don't find it, just carry on along the main path and keep moving in the same direction wherever the way becomes unclear. Eventually you will cut across the higher path. In any event, the destination is the combe above and ahead, keeping the beck on your left.

4 The path arrives at Blea Water next to the small dam on the outflow beck. From here, look in the direction of the footpath that follows the northern shore. At an angle of 45 degrees to the right is the route upwards towards the ridge of Riggindale and Rough Crags, heading for Caspel Gate. This path is not immediately apparent, but can just be discerned 20yds (18m) away at the top of a small knoll, so ignore the more obvious paths around here.

5 From the knoll, the path is clearer for a short distance as it rises over grass. When it again becomes indistinct, follow the darker patches of grass up to where the way appears to fork.

6 At this point, look along the right fork, upon which a small cairn marks the path, with another cairn shortly after it. A path can clearly be seen above it. It appears to be the uppermost reaches of the path you are on, but is in fact part of the ridge path that runs along Caspel Gate. After a steep ascent of about 15 minutes, you will arrive abruptly at it.

7 Turn left. The stone and shale path rises to the west along the sharp spur of Long Stile, and emerges onto the plateau of High Street at a point marked by a large cairn.

Continued over page

8 Suddenly the outlook changes completely, flattening out with a covering of grass. There is no path now, but walk directly forward (west) for about 50yd (45m) and a stone wall appears another 50yd (45m) ahead. If you want to visit the fell summit, turn left along the wallside path for about three minutes until you reach the triangulation column.

9 On returning, you can recognise the point at which you first met the wall by two tiny cairns that branch away to the right, pointing towards the now unseen cairn above Long Stile. Cross the tumbledown wall and proceed at right angles to it (west), to arrive at High Street.

10 The route now goes to the right (north).

11 Ten minutes along the way, the track is joined from the right by the wall. Cross it again, emerging on the edge of the ridge at the southern end of the Straits of Riggindale.

12 Now on the eastern side of the wall, High Street continues up and northwards until it reaches a cairn where it branches to the right, heading for Kidsty Pike.

13 Before it reaches the Pike, the path of the Roman road fades to the left, whilst our way is straight on along the more obvious path over the Pike.

14 After the summit this becomes indistinct, but continues in the same direction and after a short descent the way is once again clear. As the path approaches the two knolls of Kidsty Howes, it drops steeply and changes underfoot from grass to stone and shale.

15 When the ground opens out on the grassy lower slopes, head for the stone hump bridge that can be seen over Randale Beck.

16 Don't cross the bridge but turn right just before it and follow the stone path to the footbridge over Riggindale Beck.

17 Once over the footbridge, a faint track in the field bisects the angle of the main path on the left and the beck on the right. Follow this track across to a gap in the wall in the far right-hand corner of the field.

18 Through the gap, a path runs alongside the wall up to the eagle hide.

19 Return along the side of the wall down past the gap until you regain the main path.

20 Turn right up towards the wooded Rigg.

21 Close to the trees the path passes through a gate and then drops down alongside the reservoir.

22 Follow the path that skirts the waterside to return to the car park.

10.15pm. The last day of June. Haweswater reflects the fading sky, viewed from Harter Fell

SMALL WATER AND HARTER FELL

Once again starting from Mardale, our surroundings on all sides are high, rugged peaks as Haweswater slips slowly behind Artle Crag. The High Street range grows prominent to our rear and the long ridges of Rough Crag and Kidsty Pike sweep down towards the lake. Later, when more height has been gained and Haweswater comes back into sight, the view extends past the lake's immediate surroundings to include the north-eastern plains and beyond to the Pennines. To the south, the great, green valley of Longsleddale seems to stretch to infinity.

Shortly before arriving on the summit of Harter Fell, there is a curious patch of ground on which stands a large cairn. Here, the rocks protrude through a thin layer of vegetation like hundreds of jagged teeth, as if some unseen hand has arranged them so. The rocky summit itself is quite broad, making it necessary to walk a few paces across the plateau in order to look down the length of Haweswater. At 2,552ft (778m) this summit marks the highest point of the walk. Soon after leaving, the finest panorama of the day unfolds.

The outlook above the Nan Bield Pass is simply awesome, looking down on the handiwork of the ice ages. To the left are the stark, soaring peaks around Kentmere Reservoir. Straight ahead a series of mountain ranges stretch one after another to the far horizon. Further to the right lie the massive combes of Blea and Small Water tarns, with another backdrop of mountains.

By far the most impressive aspect of the view, however, is the sheer severity of the more immediate surroundings. Sharp, shattered rocks protrude on all sides, with yet more strewn across the ground. In the Small Water combe countless enormous boulders remain where they have rested for at least 8,000 years. Scree and stone form much of the combe walls, adding to the harsh impression.

The ancient thoroughfare of the Nan Bield Pass provides passage down to Small Water. This track was used to link Kentmere with Mardale in the days of packhorses. Three stone shelters built to protect the travellers of those times from storms still survive on the tarn's northern shore.

Small Water lies at an altitude of 1,480ft (451m). The surroundings are quite open and slope gently to the south-east of the outflow, quickly becoming steep and rocky as the eye passes clockwise around the shore. The massed rocks and boulders were carved out of Harter Fell, Small Water Crag and Piot Crag by glaciers, and a small number were made by the prising action of centuries of frost. The high walls of the combe give most of the tarn's environment an enclosed, rugged appearance. The tarn itself measures around 400yd by 200yd (360m by 180m) with a maximum depth of over 50ft (15m). Many brown trout and a few perch lurk beneath the surface. Whilst there are no record-breaking fish in this or any other tarn, a good number grow to a respectable size.

There is a series of tiny beaches and then a small welcoming bay on the southern shore. This side of the tarn is also best for camping. However, the water becomes deep very quickly from most parts of the shore, so a measure of caution is called for when bathing. That having been said, in warm weather, particularly after a long walk, there is nothing as invigorating as a swim in a high tarn. In the right conditions, the clean air, bare rock and crystal waters can combine to provide spa-like qualities.

Soon after leaving this classic tarn, a stone slab footbridge marks another captivating spot. Haweswater lies below, and across the head of the valley, Blea Water Beck crashes down to merge with Small Water's outflow and then into the lake.

The path down into the valley is a popular one, but no matter how busy it is, I find that nothing disturbs the remote, wild nature.

Overleaf: High summer sunrise over Small Water and Haweswater viewed from Mardale Ill Bell

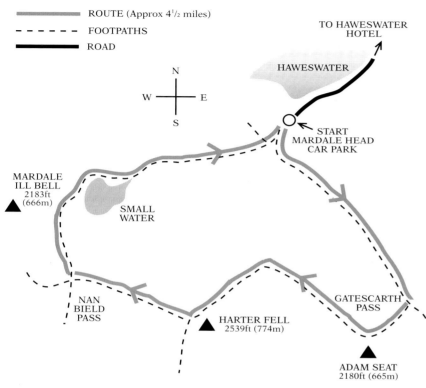

TO HAWESWATER
HOTEL

HAWESWATER

N
W   E
S

START
MARDALE HEAD
CAR PARK

MARDALE
ILL BELL
2183ft
(666m)

SMALL
WATER

NAN
BIELD
PASS

GATESCARTH
PASS

HARTER FELL
2539ft (774m)

ADAM SEAT
2180ft (665m)

ROUTE SUMMARY

MAP: OS Outdoor Leisure Map 5

START: Mardale Head car park, Haweswater, GR 469107

DISTANCE: Approximately 4½ miles (7km)

TIME: 2 – 2½ hours

DIFFICULTY: Steep descent to tarn

ROUTE DIRECTIONS

This is a particularly easy route to follow; there are very few cross-paths or branches to cause confusion. However, the ascents and descents are steep for the most part.

1 From Mardale car park, go through the gate by the triple-route metal sign, then take the first track that branches left. This heads south-east up to Gatescarth Pass. Harter Fell lies ahead, with Gatescarth Beck and then a small pine wood on the left. Height is gained quickly on the well-trodden, stony track.

2 There are two sections or steps on the initial ascent, separated by a small hanging valley. At the top of the second section, the main track goes straight on through a gate towards the contrasting rolling landscape ahead, but a few paces before this, our path branches off sharply to the right and upwards heading west.

3 The final ascent up to Harter Fell's summit begins now. The gradient remains quite steep as Haweswater reappears to the right.

4 Little Harter Fell comes next and then a cairn as the ground becomes rock-strewn. Shortly after the first cairn, the path arrives on the summit, marked by another large cairn intermingled with a tangled mass of old iron fencing.

5 From here carry on in the same direction (west), ignoring the path that bears left alongside a fence, as that leads to Kentmere Pike. At this point our track is unclear, but the way is marked by some small cairns.

6 As the track begins to descend gently, the Helvellyn range, with much of the central and north-western fells, can be seen ahead. The gradient becomes steeper now as the path snakes down to the hause of Nan Bield Pass. This is a major cross-path, in the centre of which will be seen a large stone shelter.

7 Turn right here to the north and go down to Small Water, a very steep and rocky descent.

8 On reaching the tarn, the path passes the old stone shelters, following the shoreline until it arrives at the outflow beck.

9 Cross the stepping stones and the path then accompanies the stream on its descent to Haweswater. This is steep for only a short while, and most of the final leg can be dealt with comfortably.

10 A little over twenty minutes after leaving Small Water you will come to the car park and journey's end.

SMALL WATER

CHAPTER 2

LANTY'S TARN
& RED TARN

HELVELLYN

Lanty's Tarn mirrors a perfectly still spring morning, looking towards Grisedale

After Windermere, England's largest lake is Ullswater in the north-east of the National Park, which is considered by many to be the most beautiful of them all. It lies where two of the three main geological formations of the region, the ancient sedimentary rocks known as Skiddaw Slate and the harder Borrowdale Volcanics, intermingle. This gives the lake a meandering course and the shores vary from gently rolling countryside to high, broken crags. Three tiny islands in the southern reaches provide constant delight for those who love to 'mess about in boats'. They are the stuff of dreams for a picnic and become treasure islands for the very young. The central one is known to some locals as 'Star Gazy Island', a favourite haunt on clear summer nights.

The National Trust owns large parcels of land around the lake including the Gowbarrow Estate with its famous Aira Force waterfall. The estate is reputed to be the location of Wordsworth's famous line 'I wandered lonely as a cloud' although there is no longer a host of golden daffodils. It is an area rich in wildlife, and ospreys have been seen here recently, but they have yet to settle. Red kites are also reported to be making a comeback.

Owing to the lack of a rail service and the difficulty of mountain roads, tourism was slow to reach Ullswater. It was only when the M6 was built within 5 miles (8km) of Pooley Bridge in 1968 that the numbers of visitors increased. Now, although it attracts a share of visitors, its environs retain a stately ambience, escaping the attention of most day-trippers. Cream teas and cucumber sandwiches are the norm here, in contrast to Windermere's hot-dogs. The unhurried pace extends to the lake, where only sail and low-powered motor boats are allowed. During the summer months just two elegant steamers satisfy the demand for pleasure cruising, plying their trade between Glenridding Pier and Pooley Bridge, 8 miles (13km) to the north. The senior vessel, the *Lady of the Lake*, was launched in 1877, followed by the *Raven* in 1889.

THE WALK

The campsite at Gillside Farm in Glenridding provides an ideal base for a spectacular circuit of mountains and tarns. Glenridding Beck dances through the trees alongside the campsite, but this cheerful stream has not always appeared so kindly. In the small hours of 30 October 1927, it was instrumental in Glenridding's darkest episode.

Up at the head of the valley at Keppel Cove, there was once a tarn, which was held in check by natural moraine. It was used by Greenside Lead Mines as a reservoir until the miners needed more water. Incredibly, they decided that the solution was to bore through the moraine, and after a night of torrential rain, this natural dam, which had done its job for thousands of years collapsed, disgorging the whole tarn down the valley via Glenridding Beck. Bridges and buildings were destroyed and the village swamped. Many animals were killed, but astonishingly no human lives were lost, despite reports of beds floating at ceiling height. One account relates the heroism of a male employee from a local inn, who after being trapped himself, subsequently rescued the maids by breaking into their sleeping quarters. Exactly how he managed to find his way through the darkness and confusion to that particular door, apparently with such practised ease, has never been fully explained.

From the southernmost reaches of Ullswater, the valleys of Patterdale, Grisedale and Glenridding sweep away, divided by high ridges. The one between Grisedale and Glenridding culminates in a crag overlooking the lake. A shallow depression or col links this crag with the main ridge, and hidden there, amid the trees is the bewitching Lanty's Tarn, the first objective of this walk.

Just minutes into the journey a fine view of Ullswater and Glenridding unfolds, expanding to include the remnants of Greenside Mines. Further along, over the hill crest, the valley sounds are left behind as one enters the silent dell of Lanty's Tarn. Located in a woodland setting at an altitude of 900ft (274m) Lanty's was originally a natural tarn. It is now partially dammed at the southern end, and its measurements fluctuate according to the rainfall. For most of the year, it is around 500ft (150m) long and is 100ft (30m) wide. A drought reduces its extent dramatically, and this is why there are no longer any fish here, save for a handful of minnows.

Ingeniously, the dam was constructed in order to create a year-round supply of ice for nearby Patterdale Hall. On winter's days the frozen surface was cut into blocks then sealed in storage chambers within the dam. The estate also stocked the water with Ullswater trout, harvesting them every summer after draining the tarn to clear the weeds. There are local whispers relating to past ungodly rituals in the surrounding woods; indeed more than one person has told me that they feel mildly uncomfortable here, but I have never found it to be anything other than peaceful and charming.

Beyond the tarn a number of Scots pines stand proudly alongside the path, and ahead across Grisedale, the bulk of Birks and St Sunday Crag looms large, dominating the skyline. The main ascent of the walk begins now as the path rises towards Bleaberry Crag. The magnificent Grisedale valley lies beneath us, flanked by St Sunday Crag's precipitous slopes. Although quite steep, the climb only becomes strenuous over the last 300yd (275m), mainly because of the loose stone and shale underfoot.

Soon the path begins to approach the Lake District's most popular feature: Striding Edge. Initially the ridge is broad, moderately rocky and marked with a series of cairns – giving no hint of what is to come. Ullswater comes into view behind and Red Tarn is unveiled ahead to the right. The ridge becomes very rocky, narrower and then suddenly arrives on the edge proper, with drops on both sides. Some 800ft (240m) below to the left lies Nethermost Cove, with Red Tarn on the right. From this position, the far section of the climb up Helvellyn's eastern face looks almost impossible to the casual walker, but when tackled it is surprisingly easy.

There are several paths along Striding Edge, one on the very crest passing directly over a series of small, sharp pinnacles. The other, safer paths are a few feet below this. Progress is slow, but this is a truly exhilarating experience for all but experienced mountaineers. The final pinnacle is the most difficult or the best fun, depending on one's mood. Then comes a scramble up the connecting slope of Helvellyn.

If it is taken slowly and with care, there is no real danger in the traverse of Striding Edge, as long as the weather holds good. However, it should not be attempted in strong winds or slippery conditions. The full crossing from Bleaberry Crag to Helvellyn's summit takes around an hour. Along the way you might notice a memorial plaque to one Robert Dixon, who died here in 1858 while following the Patterdale Fox Hounds.

The link with Striding Edge and the proximity of Red Tarn are the main reasons for Helvellyn's unsurpassed popularity among the Lakeland peaks; at 3,118ft (950m) the summit is ranked only third highest in the district. I have always thought, however, that the poetic lilt of the name holds an attraction of its own. There is no generally accepted origin for the name; it could be derived from words meaning William, hill, lake or well.

Even though the summit is broad, there is still a 360 degree view on offer here, incorporating most of the major fells. To the northeast Ullswater snakes away into the distance. If you stay overnight under clear skies, the sunrise seen from Helvellyn is not to be missed.

Close by the summit cairn, a damaged tablet commemorates a unique and quite incredible achievement by John Leeming and Bert Hinkler. On 22 December 1926, they landed an aeroplane on this peak!

They had originally chosen Snowdon for a stunt designed to demonstrate the capabilities of their Gosport aeroplane. Switching to Helvellyn after learning of its open summit, they chose two possible landing sites and cleared them of boulders. Friends were conscripted to witness the event and to light a fire as a wind direction indicator. However, mechanical problems delayed the take-off from Woodford in Cheshire and eventually forced them down near Lancaster.

The following day, when nobody was expecting them and Helvellyn was virtually deserted, they launched a successful attempt. The tiny craft landed just 10yd (9m) from the summit cairn – nowhere near the prepared strips. Fortunately for the pilots, there was one witness to verify their feat, Professor E. R. Dobbs of Birmingham University. Leeming and Hinkler had only 30yd (27m) in which to take off again, heading into the teeth of a fierce wind straight for the 800ft (240m) cliff overlooking Red Tarn. History records that they made it, somehow.

Beneath the surface of the tarn lies another plane that wasn't so lucky. During World War II many British bombers used the shining surfaces of the lakes as beacons in the night to guide them to their home bases in Lancashire. Looking for Ullswater, this plane strayed too far west and crashed into Striding Edge. Investigators salvaged some items and then tipped the remains into the water.

There is another plaque on Helvellyn in memory of a young man named Charles Gough, who was killed in a fall here. Last seen on 18 April 1805, his body wasn't discovered until 20 July, an event that caused massive interest owing to the fact that his pet spaniel was still faithfully in attendance, guarding his remains. Both Sir Walter Scott and Wordsworth were moved to commemorate this loyalty in verse.

The steep, rocky path on Swirral Edge is the way down from here. Although it lacks the inspirational qualities of its neighbour,

Striding Edge, this is still a very impressive feature and it requires a measure of caution to negotiate it. The first 200ft (60m) or so of the descent is literally a scramble. Way below to the left lies Brown Cove and further on is Keppel Cove. Both were formerly the sites of small tarns that have disappeared, the assorted debris of old mine workings now take their places. The path becomes more comfortable as it nears the tarn, but first you may want to take the slight detour up to the pinnacle of Catstye Cam; the views are certainly rewarding.

Eventually the path arrives at Red Tarn's outflow, at an altitude of 2,350ft (716m). The remnants of a dam built in 1860 are still very much in evidence here. Another large tarn, it measures 550yd by 300yd (500m by 275m) and has a maximum depth of over 80ft (25m). Once again the water here is wonderfully clear and contains large numbers of wily brown trout that share their home with schelly, a rare silvery fish that is otherwise found only in Ullswater and Haweswater. They usually lie very deep, and are difficult but not impossible to catch. Wordsworth often fished in this, the highest trout water in England.

The surrounding ground falls sharply to the tarn on three sides, opening out by the outflow to the north-east. The slope continues steeply beneath the surface on the southern and south-western sides. On the north-western shore two small bays offer safer, shallower water for young bathers. The tarn basin was scooped out of solid rock by its glaciers, which then deposited enormous quantities of boulders to form the containing moraine, through which the outflow beck wanders.

Of all the tarns, this has the most awe-inspiring setting. The giant bulk of Helvellyn forms the back wall, flanked by the towering, serrated arêtes of Striding Edge and Swirral Edge. The distinctive point of Catstye Cam climbs above and beyond Swirral Edge, adding to the majestic prospect. This is a place to linger for hours, soaking

Red Tarn from Helvellyn. The summer sun rises
beyond distant Ullswater

lure of a potentially deserted mountain combe proved irresistible. However, my peace was shattered when I arrived to find that many people had had the same idea. I couldn't see them but their sounds were all around, eerily accentuated by the mist.

All that remains of the walk is the return to Glenridding. The path descends alongside Red Tarn Beck, passing close by the numerous cascades. The beck merges with outflows from Keppel Cove and widens in the deeper part of the valley to become Glenridding Beck. Here the remnants of Greenside Mines occupy the opposite hillside.

During the nineteenth century these mines were very successful, and the greater part of Glenridding village was constructed during the boom years. It wasn't until 1960 that they closed for the last time. Just before they closed, tests on seismic equipment led to the deaths of two miners, only the second fatal accident in the long history of Greenside. In the valley above the workings there used to be another tarn, fed by Sticks Gill. As at Keppel Cove, the outflow was dammed to accommodate the mines but since their closure the water has been allowed to run free, and now little remains but marshes.

The course of Glenridding Beck forms a deep gorge as the path carries on down the valley and passes the youth hostel. Ullswater reappears ahead and then comes a bird's eye view of Glenridding and Gillside Farm. Now the descent is steep for the short distance that remains until the path deposits us gently in the heart of the campsite. The Traveller's Rest, a popular watering hole, is just five minutes' walk from here and provides a restful atmosphere in which to reflect on the day's or weekend's activities. Down in the village, the Hikers' Bar at the Ullswater Hotel caters for the younger element who may still have some energy, while Ratcher's Tavern at the Glenridding Hotel offers a happy medium. For details of the large variety of accommodation in Glenridding, call the Tourist Information Office on 017684 82414.

up the clean, wholesome atmosphere. I remember one particularly hot, tiring day when I arrived here and trudged gratefully into the water. After just a few minutes' swimming I was so invigorated that I promptly went back up Helvellyn, not by way of any paths but by the almost sheer eastern face.

Camping by Red Tarn is an absolute delight, with many comfortable locations around the shore. You will never be alone here. Once I visited the tarn during a complete white-out, with unbroken cloud and mist blanketing everything from the peak summits to the valleys; it is not wise to venture out under those conditions but the

Above: A misty autumn morning on Helvellyn, looking south-west to the Langdales and distant Coniston Fells

ROUTE DIRECTIONS

The Gillside Farm campsite lies a few hundred yards up the road that climbs through Glenridding village towards Greenside's old lead mines.

1 Leave the site on the path by the beck, heading downstream.

2 Two minutes along the way there is a signpost and a path that forks sharply right, away from the beck. At first glance the sign doesn't appear very helpful – there's nothing on it. However a look on its opposite side reveals the inscription 'Lanty's Tarn/Helvellyn', and this is the route to take.

3 Pass through some gateposts marked by yellow direction indicators, and you arrive at a footbridge and a small gate, with a sign marked 'Grisedale/Helvellyn'.

4 After this the path rises steeply to another gate, an erosion control detour. Follow the sign pointing to 'Lanty's Tarn/Striding Edge'.

5 Just before yet another gate, the path branches to the left, the sign to follow here says 'Striding Edge/Grisedale'. This leads to Lanty's Tarn.

6 On leaving the tarn, the route descends beside the outflow beck.

7 A stream cuts across the path, which then forks towards two gates. Take the upper one.

8 Through the gate are three paths. One goes sharp left, another straight on and ours branches to the right up the hillside.

9 After passing through two gates on the climb to Hole-in-the-Wall, you will be faced with two stiles. Take the small one on your left, which leads to Bleaberry Crag.

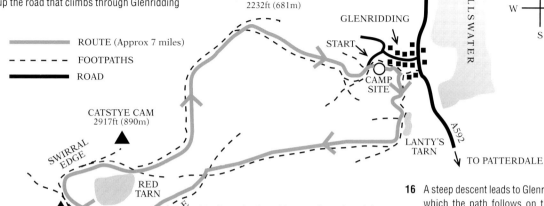

10 Follow the cairns to Striding Edge. Here one can choose between the crest itself or the slightly lower and easier paths.

11 Once across the edge there comes the scramble up Helvellyn. There are various paths on this section, all of which lead up towards the summit. Perhaps it is best to bear right wherever possible on this ascent, although you may find it more comfortable some other way.

12 On Helvellyn turn right (north-west) following the ridge of Red Tarn's combe, then go down to the tarn by way of Swirral Edge. This forms the opposite wall of the combe from Striding Edge and is the first path you will see on your right (north-east).

13 After the initial scramble down Swirral Edge, the path branches left to Catstye Cam.

14 Come back to this same branch and then continue down to the tarn, passing a cairn where the path peters out a few yards before reaching the outflow beck.

15 To leave Red Tarn go back to the cairn and walk to the north-east, roughly half-way between the outflow gully and the slope of Catstye Cam. The path is barely visible here, but follow the darker patches of peat, looking for footprints. These worn areas approach the gully, where the path becomes obvious, stony and dry.

16 A steep descent leads to Glenridding Beck, which the path follows on the right.

17 Opposite Greenside Mines, the main track crosses the beck, but stay on your present side, bearing to the right.

18 Eventually the path reaches a steep rock outcrop overlooking Glenridding. With the rock face immediately to your right, look down to the left and locate the path that branches down. Take it through the ferns to a gate and stile.

19 Cross the stile onto the farm track and go down to the campsite.

ROUTE SUMMARY

MAP:	OS Outdoor Leisure Map 5
START:	Gillside Farm campsite, Glenridding GR 379169
DISTANCE:	Approximately 7 miles (11km)
TIME:	4 – 4½ hours
DIFFICULTY:	High level route. Care must be taken on Striding and Swirral Edges. Not for beginners

LANTY'S TARN AND RED TARN

CHAPTER 3

PATTERDALE

On the route through Hartsop Hamlet in autumn, looking south

The great glacier that formed Ullswater reached down from the mountains through what is now the verdant valley of Patterdale. With magnificent surroundings of high rugged peaks contrasting with the rich pasture lands, this is a popular attraction for those who wish to enjoy 'alpine' scenery without having to climb.

The area is particularly pleasant in the autumn when the russet and gold of the fells and their woods complement the dominant greens of the fields. It is fitting therefore, that the valley should be named after Patrick, patron saint of the Emerald Isle, who is reputed to have passed through here. A well that bears his name can be found by the roadside at the northern end of the dale, adjacent to the southern reaches of Ullswater.

Up at the head of the valley is the famous Kirkstone Pass. This name is derived from an old Norse word and refers to the huge, church-like rock that stands at the top of the pass. At 1,476ft (450m), Kirkstone is the highest of the Lakeland passes that carry roads, but is easier to negotiate than some others, such as the notorious Hardknott Pass for example. Before the construction of the M6 motorway provided access from the north-east, Kirkstone was the main gateway into the heart of the fells and valleys of the region, which explains why this most unlikely of locations was chosen as the site for an inn which stands near the Kirkstone itself. This thriving establishment has surprised and delighted travellers for almost 500 years.

As is to be expected in such a well-managed and conserved area, much of the land is controlled by the National Trust. Patterdale's small lake, Brotherswater, also belongs to them. The welcoming Brotherswater Inn stands on the roadside above the lake, close to a well-appointed campsite.

A couple of sleepy hamlets nestle amongst the fields and it is from the most northerly, itself named Patterdale, that the first of two walks from the valley begins.

GRISEDALE TARN

There is a car park opposite the Patterdale Hotel, and one in front of the hotel itself which is reserved for patrons. The route begins at the rear of the building on a grassy path that runs through a small copse.

Above here, there used to be a cannon, mounted on one of the crags for the entertainment of visitors during the 1830s. Occasionally, it was fired to demonstrate the amazing acoustics of the area as the echoes reverberated around the fells. This phenomenon was also demonstrated on Ullswater during the previous century, with the cannons mounted on boats.

After crossing a stream and passing through the sparsely wooded lower slopes, the first ascent of the day begins in earnest as the path heads up towards Birks. A good way up the steep incline there is a very welcome grassy ledge that offers a chance to rest and enjoy the splendid view of Ullswater with its bustling pier. Soon we gain the highest point of the path along Birks and from here both mighty Helvellyn and Striding Edge enter the panorama.

The route continues along Birks with Grisedale below to the right. So soon into the walk, considerable height has already been gained, and there is a real sense of being far out onto the fells as the path picks its way over the undulating ground.

Various streams cross the way, flowing down from Birks summit on the left, and these cause the odd patches of marsh which have to be skirted. However, this does not detract from the enjoyment of the walk, as the gradually expanding views constantly refresh one's enthusiasm.

The towering 'sugar loaf' image of St Sunday Crag lies directly ahead. This looks a daunting prospect, but it is a curious anomaly of fell walking that the steep climbs are often easily conquered, whilst the long, gradual slopes require greater effort. This ascent of around

A summer morning on St Sunday Crag, looking north-east to Grisedale and Ullswater

25

650ft (200m) is quickly rewarded when we reach a point where the path emerges from an outcrop of striated rocks and flattens out considerably. Now the views are simply glorious. To the west is the Helvellyn massif and to the north-east Grisedale with Ullswater, while to the east Angle Tarn nestles above Patterdale with a backdrop of peaks and ridges that mark the course of High Street's Roman road.

The path remains distinct across St Sunday's stony plateau, and then suddenly Grisedale Tarn is revealed ahead, resplendent in its mountain throne. On this section the near side of Grisedale is obscured by the lip of the mountain, and it is tempting to cross the few yards to the right and sneak a look straight down into the valley. But I strongly advise against doing this, as there are loose stones underfoot, followed by a 1,000ft (300m) cliff. The summit of St Sunday Crag 2,759ft (841m) is slightly to the east of the path and a five minute detour is required to visit it.

Next comes the descent to Deepdale Hause, a narrow ridge linking St Sunday Crag with Cofa Pike. Passing along the crest, an almost sheer drop opens out on the right, then on the left, offering a view down the length of Deepdale. In the deepest part of the hause, a path runs down to the right, heading for Grisedale Tarn. But don't be tempted by this, for the finest viewpoint of the day is yet to come.

Carry on to the sharp pinnacle of Cofa Pike, where a series of four mountain ridges are seen sweeping down towards Ullswater. Later, on Fairfield's wide open and rocky summit there are numerous cairns and stone shelters if you should need them, and on all sides there is scenery to take your breath away. At 2,864ft (873m) this marks the apex of the walk.

The plateau is so expansive that one could easily spend a couple of hours exploring the multitude of views on offer. On three sides, long valleys fall away, with Deepdale flanked by some spectacular jagged peaks. To the south, both Windermere and Coniston are taken in with just one glance. Beyond Seat Sandal to the west, the bulk of the Central Fells fill the horizon.

The very steep path from Fairfield to Grisedale Tarn descends through 1,100ft (340m), yet standing by the shore one is still 1,768ft (539m) above sea level. The tarn sits proudly at the head of the great Grisedale valley which was formed by the largest glacier in Lakeland. Roughly pear-shaped, the tarn measures about 600yd by 330yd (548m by 300m). Fed by inlet streams from Seat Sandal and Dollywaggon Pike, it boasts clean, clear water and contains many brown trout, perch and eels. With a maximum depth of over 100ft (30m) this is one of the deeper tarns. Families of mallards are often seen here, pursuing minnows and fry around the shallows by the outflow beck. The shoreline is accessible all the way around, and the water becomes deep quickly.

Fairfield, Seat Sandal and Dollywaggon Pike soar away from the waterside. Being widely separated, they present a strong throne-like picture with the tarn as the seat, Fairfield and Dollywaggon the arms and Seat Sandal the backrest. Another recurring image is that of a giant three-pronged crown, an impression that lends itself to the tarn's most celebrated legend.

Around the year 940, the Celtic King Domhnall of Cumbria was something of a thorn in the side of Edmund, King of England. Despite having sworn allegiance to Edmund, Domhnall plotted with rebels of Viking descent against him. For a long time Edmund had harboured secret desires to possess Domhnall's crown, which was reputed to be charmed, guaranteeing succession to the wearer.

Domhnall's treachery gave Edmund the excuse he had been looking for and he promptly dispatched his forces to crush the Celts. After a long, hard battle Domhnall was slain by traitors within his own army, but his dying wish was that the crown should be kept safe. A group of his closest aides managed to break through the

Right: The clouds break on a wild spring day to reveal Grisedale Tarn, viewed from St Sunday Crag

The path over Cofa Pike, viewed from Fairfield in high summer. Striding Edge and Helvellyn form the central horizon

enemy ranks and escaped to Grisedale Tarn, where they consigned the crown to the depths.

Nowadays, a little over a mile to the west of the tarn stands a large cairn at Dunmail Raise, which commemorates the spot where Domhnall fell. One night each year, a spectral band of his followers is said to return to the tarn, ensuring that the crown remains hidden and waiting for the return of its true owner. It is a hauntingly romantic tale, sadly refuted by some historians who maintain that Domhnall died at a later date whilst on pilgrimage to Rome.

Grisedale Tarn more or less represents the half-way mark on this walk, and logically a good spot to camp, especially as there are many places where a tent could be pitched on the grassy surround. But owing to the wide dispersal of the perimeter peaks, it can be very windy, so be sure to check the weather forecast before starting out.

The path along the shore is part of the ancient pack horse route that linked Grasmere with Patterdale. We follow it now past the outflow and begin the walk down into Grisedale. A few paces into the descent, about 30yd (27m) to the right of the path, a small rusted sign can be seen on top of a large rock. This marks the spot of one of Lakeland's numerous sites of interest for Wordsworth enthusiasts, and the well-trodden ground around the rock base is testimony to his undying popularity. In 1888 the rock was inscribed in memory of the final meeting between the poet and his brother John, and is known as the Brothers' Parting Stone.

John was the captain of the largest merchant ship owned by the East India Company. Although something of a poet himself, he concentrated on more worldly matters, promising to keep William and their sister Dorothy comfortable financially while William got on with the business of being a genius. But in 1805 John's ship the *Earl of Abergavenny* sank on the Shambles just off the Dorset coast, and he was drowned. Reports at the time blamed the incompetence of the pilot. William was devastated at the news, apparently unable to come to terms with the fact that his beloved brother could have perished so close to the safety of the shore.

Like many other parts of Lakeland, Grisedale has a history of mining. The route takes us past Ruthwaite Lodge, now a climbing hut restored by the Outward Bound organisation. Before that it was used as a shooting lodge, but originally it was a mine building. Further down the valley at Eagle Crag are the remains of another mine. Both date back to Elizabethan times.

Soon the path crosses a footbridge over Grisedale Beck, then drops gradually into the valley basin. St Sunday Crag towers so high above that it is literally a neck-craning prospect. Surprisingly, it gives an even stronger sense of height now than it did before, when we looked down from it. The array of crags and cliffs just below the top path can all be seen clearly. Dollywaggon Pike, High Crag and Nethermost Pike are behind us, while Bleaberry Crag and Grisedale Brow rise up on the far side of the valley beyond the fields of grazing cows and sheep. This is one of the best loved Lakeland valleys and the walking is a joy along the easy farm tracks. At one time the dale was densely forested and a favourite place for hunters of wild boar. The name Grisedale means 'Valley of the Pigs'.

Our way enters a wooded area towards the end of the valley, with the deep gorge of Grisedale Beck on the left. With tarmac underfoot now, we pass some cottages and then descend into Patterdale, skirting around the sports fields before arriving back at the Patterdale Hotel.

The walk covers about 8½ miles (13.5km), and there is some hard work involved on the ascents. But the only part that could be described as difficult is the very steep descent from Fairfield to Grisedale Hause. I strongly recommend this route for lovers of mountain scenery – there are few ranges that can match the grandeur of the Birks to Fairfield section and the sense of freedom that it bestows.

Overleaf: A summer morning on Fairfield. Great Rigg and Rydal Fell lead on to Windermere (left), Esthwaite Water (centre), Coniston Water and the sea

ROUTE DIRECTIONS

1 From the car park facing the Patterdale Hotel, go to the right, around the back of the hotel and you will find a sign saying 'Public Footpath'.

2 The path forks immediately; go right on the narrow track through a copse. Pass through the first gate and carry on past two faint right forks. This leads to another gate marked 'Footpath'.

3 After this, the way arrives at a cross-path. Turn left here up the steep slope to Birks.

4 A climb of around 15 minutes leads to a wall and stile, after which the path skirts to the right (west) of Birks summit. Stay on the ridge, ignoring the path that branches down to the right.

5 St Sunday Crag is the next objective. It is unmistakable and lies directly ahead (south-west). A path from Birks summit joins from the left and just after this the ascent begins. The path often divides, but it doesn't matter which one you take as they all lead to the correct place. Once you gain the St Sunday plateau, the path is marked by a series of cairns.

6 Then comes the descent to Deepdale Hause. Ignore the paths that lead off it to the right and carry on straight up Cofa Pike.

7 Between Cofa Pike and Fairfield, another path forks right and down to Grisedale Tarn, but our way is straight on to Fairfield.

8 At the first cairn you see, the path forks. Take the left fork up to Fairfield summit.

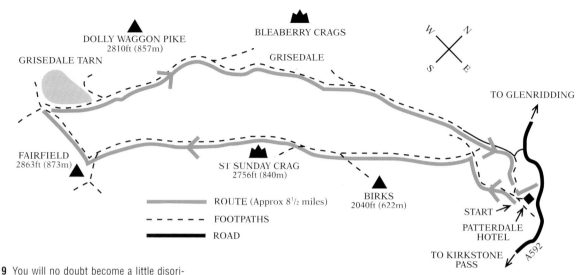

9 You will no doubt become a little disorientated after sampling Fairfield's views. Take a compass reading and head due west. The path down to Grisedale Tarn is marked by a series of cairns. It is extremely steep and composed of loose stone and shale.

10 Eventually you will reach a cross-path by the ruined wall on Grisedale Hause. Turn right here down to the tarn.

11 Follow the path along the shore and cross the outflow beck.

12 Bear right into Grisedale.

13 After Ruthwaite Lodge the track forks left over a footbridge; do not cross this but go to the right, staying on the present side of the stream.

14 Down in the valley basin, another farm track goes to the left, off our track. Ignore this and carry on down the valley.

15 The lane drops down past some cottages and then curves to the left. Here the track splits into three. Take the central one signposted 'Public Footpath'.

16 This path leads to some yellow direction markers. Cross the stile at the markers and continue to follow them across the undulating ground until they lead to a white-tipped post next to a wall on your right.

17 Cross the wall stile and turn left, after which the path leads down to the Patterdale Hotel.

ROUTE SUMMARY

MAP:	OS Outdoor Leisure Map 5
START:	Patterdale Hotel, GR 395159
DISTANCE:	Approximately 8½ miles (13.5km)
TIME:	4½ – 5 hours
DIFFICULTY:	High level route. Steep climbs and one extremely steep descent. Not for beginners

ANGLE TARN

The second walk from Patterdale is a shorter one and does not include any high peaks. The total ascent amounts to only 1,300ft (395m) from the level of Patterdale and 2½ hours should be sufficient to cover a route that visits one of Lakeland's most beautiful tarns. The ascent is long but broken by level sections, so legs and lungs do not have to work very hard. Anglers should visit Beckstones Farm for a fishing permit before venturing out. While there, parents and children will have the opportunity to feed an orphan lamb.

After leaving the main road through Patterdale, the route continues on tarmac along a lane moving parallel with the course of the valley. Green pastures on our left lead to the western ridges, whilst high crags tower above immediately on our right. Livestock graze contentedly in the fields beside the lane, and you will find it difficult to set anything more than a relaxed pace, in keeping with the peaceful rustic scene. Tarmac gives way to loose stone underfoot as the way passes by a group of holiday chalets. Then a wooded section clears on our right, where a precipitous gully stream cascades down the fellside. The stream's source is Angle Tarn, our main destination. Soon the path begins to rise and Patterdale grows ever longer beneath us. Ullswater appears ahead and Brotherswater to the rear. Before long the whole valley is unveiled, together with a view of Deepdale and all the fells around it.

The initial ascent leads to Boredale Hause, a col linking various ridges where at least five major footpaths converge. It is a favourite spot for lunch breaks and rest periods before walkers set out again for all points of the compass. In hot weather the stream that runs through here is put to very good use replenishing canteens and soothing fevered brows. Some people are wary of drinking from mountain streams. You will have gathered by now that I am not.

There cannot be many in Lakeland that I have not tasted, and I offer my continued existence as proof of their benign properties. However, it is always prudent to drink from where the flow is swift. White water tumbling over rocks has the finest quality, especially when the stream has travelled only a short distance from underground. If you should find such a spot, you will discover a nectar far superior to anything from tap or bottle.

The route continues to rise after Boredale Hause and then comes to a very exciting section where the path forms a narrow ledge across a steep grassy hillside. The valley lies far below, and Brotherswater most takes the eye; it is the best view of our journey. Soon after this the path skirts around Angletarn Pikes to reveal suddenly the day's principal reward lying beneath us at an altitude of 1,572ft (479m). It is curious, but no matter how often one visits a tarn, that first sighting always has an element of surprise.

Angle Tarn nestles in a shallow recess on a ridge between Angletarn Pikes, Cat Crag and Buck Crags. Its position on the ridge means that there are no high enclosing walls and the surface of the water is largely open to the sky. To north and south the ridge continues on its way while to east and west steep slopes fall down to the valleys. The outflow stream that we passed in Patterdale escapes down the western side.

It is unusual to find a ridge tarn with the proportions of Angle Tarn. Of the type, this is surely the finest. It measures approximately 400yd (370m) from north to south and 270yd (250m) from east to west at the widest point. It is difficult to give more accurate figures because of the complex character of the shore, which offers a succession of bays, peninsulas and promontories. With the possible exception of Sprinkling Tarn, I don't think there is another one that has such an interesting shoreline as this.

One can approach the water with ease from the north and east.

The west also provides easy access, apart from one small section where a crag comes down steeply. However, skirting around this leads to yet more accessible parts of the shore. From the south access is blocked by a mass of reeds and some marshy ground.

Above: A summer morning at Angle Tarn looking west beyond Patterdale to the Helvellyn range with the distinctive pinnacle of Catstye Cam

The maximum depth of the water is about 30ft (9m). It is wonderfully clear and contains pike, perch, brown trout and eels. It comes as no surprise to learn that the name 'Angle' is derived from old Norse and means 'the fishing tarn'. Two small islands lie close to the eastern shore in relatively shallow water: the fish seem to be most active around these islands and the north-eastern promontory. They are notoriously difficult to catch though, and many an angler has been driven to distraction by their speed and cunning. The surface ripples caused by the fish as they pick off flies are an incredible sight. Sometimes it appears as if rain is falling over the whole tarn. This spectacle is greatly enhanced on clear evenings when shadows creep up from the valleys and the sun reflects off the glittering water. At such times it is worth keeping a silent vigil from some darkened nook where the shores can be seen clearly. You might be rewarded by a visit from one or more of the red deer that stray up here occasionally from their grazing grounds in the north-eastern valleys.

The open outlook of the tarn provides stunning scenery. To the west St Sunday Crag and the Helvellyn range can be seen beyond the void formed by Patterdale. To the south High Street sweeps across the skyline to Gray Crag followed by Stony Cove Pike and Hartsop Dodd. This southern aspect looks particularly impressive late in the day. The low sun illuminates only the western slopes while shadows fill every cranny, showing up the mountains' course in stark detail.

Every passer-by is captivated by the beauty of Angle Tarn. Some go no further, spending the whole day exploring the shorelines and swimming from there to the islands. Others break their journey to enjoy the scene. I have even seen fell runners stop, seeming to have forgotten their tight schedules as they pause to savour the tranquillity of this enchanting place.

There is no doubt that you will be tempted to stay the night here. The northern and eastern shores provide many comfortable locations, although you might prefer other sites. Remember that if you choose the eastern side, you will have the bonus of looking across the gleaming surface into the sunset.

When you can finally drag yourself away, the path leads up to the rocky knolls on Satura Crag and then passes by Brock Crags on the descent back to Patterdale. Hayeswater Tarn comes into view to the south-east, resting in a deep basin between High Street and the towering cone shape of Gray Crag. I considered including it in the route, but as it has long been in service as a reservoir serving Penrith, swimming is prohibited. The fishing is private, and although the tarn's setting looks very compelling from our viewpoint below Satura Crag, at the waterside it takes on a banal appearance. Add all this to the fact that our only logical approach would be over a horribly muddy section, and you will understand why Hayeswater stays off the menu.

The southern aspect remains very impressive as our path continues in its descent above Hayeswater Gill. Between Gray Crag and Hartsop Dodd lies the long sweep of Pasture Bottom. Some disused mine workings are dotted around the mouth of the valley, and although a footpath leads through its course this is a little-visited area. Buzzards and kestrels are usually in evidence there, circling high above the silent valley and sombre peaks.

As our path curves round to the north, a narrow view of Patterdale and Brotherswater gradually expands and then we look down on Hartsop hamlet. A steep descent through the woods follows, after which the path enters Hartsop. Its name is derived from Old English and means 'the hill of the deer'. This is a genuinely rustic little settlement constructed entirely of Lakeland slate and stone. It exists purely as a living part of the farming community and there is no evidence of pandering to the requirements of tourists. At one time it was a busy outpost of the mining and quarrying industries, but now it dozes quietly.

The hamlet is the last port of call on our route. All that remains now is a short stroll to the main road and back to the car park.

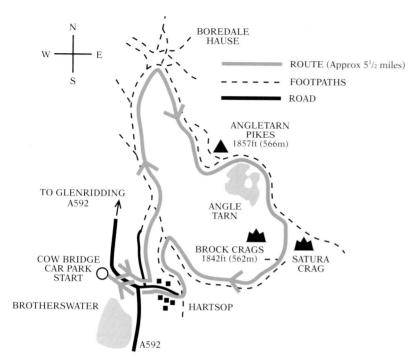

W — N — E — S (compass)

BOREDALE HAUSE

═══ ROUTE (Approx 5½ miles)
– – – FOOTPATHS
▬▬▬ ROAD

ANGLETARN PIKES
1857ft (566m)

TO GLENRIDDING
A592

ANGLE TARN

COW BRIDGE CAR PARK START

BROCK CRAGS
1842ft (562m)

SATURA CRAG

BROTHERSWATER

HARTSOP

A592

ROUTE SUMMARY

MAP: OS Outdoor Leisure Map 5

START: Cow Bridge car park, Patterdale, GR 402134

DISTANCE: Approximately 5½ miles (9km)

TIME: 2¼ – 2¾ hours

DIFFICULTY: Steep descent, otherwise comfortable

SPECIAL NEEDS: Fishing permit for tarn, available from Beckstones Farm, Patterdale

ROUTE DIRECTIONS

Cow Bridge car park is situated 1 mile (1.5km) north of Sykeside campsite and the Brotherswater Inn.

1 From the car park cross the road onto the footpath and turn right (south).

2 About 300yd (275m) along the road you will come to a minor road on your left signposted 'Hartsop ¼'. Take this road and then turn left again almost immediately at the lane signposted 'Public Bridleway' and 'Hartsop Fold'. This leads to a gate and footbridge across Angle Tarn Beck.

3 From there carry straight on to where the bridleway forks and then take the right branch up the hillside. After a moderately steep climb you will arrive slightly below Boredale Hause where a branch goes to the left.

4 Continue to your right at this point up to the hause.

5 A number of paths converge here. Ignore all the other paths and bear constantly to your right. On the extreme right you will see a path that crosses the stream. Take this one away from the hause, heading south.

6 Approximately ¾ mile further, a footbridge marks the spot where the path forks. Take the right branch that leads across the grassy hillside. Eventually both paths converge but the right branch is the far more interesting. This leads to Angle Tarn. The path continues on the eastern side and climbs up to Satura Crag.

7 Here you will be faced by a wall with a gate, and a stile to the right of the gate. Look sharp right and you will see a faint track dropping down on your side of the wall. Take this

down to a gap in the wall. To ensure that you are in the correct place you can see an old gatepost in the gap.

8 Through this the faint track appears to fork. Take the more obvious branch to the right that leads to a tumbledown wall. The general idea is to continue in a south-south-easterly direction and pick up the path below Brock Crags. But it is much simpler at this point to cross the scattered stones of the old wall and then follow the line of the wall downhill.

9 After about 100yd (90m) this drops steeply into a deep gully where you will see a faint track cutting across the gully stream. Turn sharp right here following the contour of the hillside. The track grows increasingly obvious and soon a clear path lies underfoot. Eventually this arrives at a fence and then bears to the right alongside it.

10 After this ignore the gate you come to on your left, and pass through the one ahead of you.

11 Cross over a stream and go straight on past a stone tablet. Then the path drops very steeply through woods.

12 Another path cuts across the way. Turn left on to it and you will arrive at some cottages, after which the path widens into a major track. This descends to the minor road that runs through Hartsop hamlet.

13 Turn right on the road and pass through Hartsop down to the main road.

14 Turn right here to return to the car park.

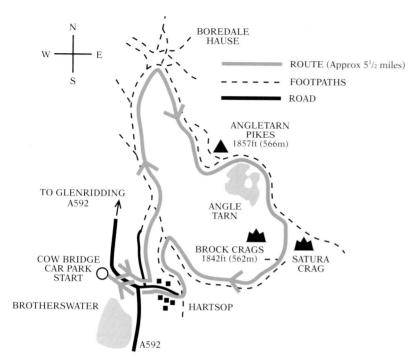

ANGLE TARN PATTERDALE

CHAPTER 4

BOWSCALE TARN

Bowscale Tarn from Bowscale Fell, looking towards Tarn Crags and Mosedale

Right: Fading light on a summer evening at Bowscale Tarn, looking towards the outflow from Bowscale Fell

St Mungo (also know as St Kentigern) wandered the northern lands of Britain during the sixth century, preaching the Christian word. His mission brought him to a scattered community of tiny hamlets in the valley due east of Blencathra's massif. A church was constructed as a result of St Mungo's ministry, and the valley, which at that time was known as Grisedale, adopted his name and became Mungrisedale.

Mungrisedale village lies at the very feet of the mountains, and provides a base for the route to Bowscale Tarn. This is the most northerly of the routes, and at Bowscale Tarn we are at the northernmost point. The walk can be done in about two and a half hours, discounting rest periods, with one long ascent to Bowscale Fell, after which it is downhill all the way. The descent into Bowscale Tarn's combe is quite precarious in places, but not very difficult. On the sections immediately before and after Bowscale Fell's summit the way cannot be seen on the ground, so do not forget your compass.

This is a remote and very quiet area, ideal for those who want to sample fells and tarns away from the crowds of central Lakeland. At the journey's end the Mill Inn is handily placed to provide refreshments. A few yards north of the inn there is an old-style red telephone box with a small parking area in front of Bannerdale Cottage. From here a track passes through farm buildings shaded by trees, and then out into an open valley between the hills.

THE WALK

Immediately, we are greeted by a blaze of heather on Scale Fell's eastern arm, which lies ahead and to the right. Our wide and stony track follows the River Glenderamackin upstream, initially heading straight for the eastern end of a long ridge known as the Tongue that sweeps down from Bowscale Fell. Then it curves to the left and begins to rise up the Tongue's southern flank.

We are only a matter of minutes into the journey, but the starting point is in such a remote setting that our track is already passing through unfenced, wide-open fell country. The valley gently rises to the south-west between Bannerdale and Souther Fell, a mountain that provides the most mystifying legend of the whole Lake District. There are many accounts of the events that occurred here in the eighteenth century, some of them contradictory. One version even places them on Blencathra, but the others generally agree on the main points:

About an hour before dark on Midsummer Eve 1735, a servant at Blake Hill's Farm, near Souther Fell, saw an army of men marching out of an outcrop on the northern tip of the fell and proceeding across the eastern side of the ridge after which they disappeared into a cleft on the summit. He claimed that the march continued for over an hour, a constant stream of soldiers that appeared very distinct,

but nobody believed him. Two years later, again on Midsummer Eve, his master, William Lancaster, was returning home at 8 o'clock in the evening. He noticed some men following their horses along the same eastern side of the fell, but taking them for a hunting party he took little notice. Ten minutes later he looked up to the fell again and saw that the men were now mounted, marshalling a long line of soldiers marching five abreast. He dashed into the farm and called out his family and servants, who all saw the same thing.

For the next eight years William Lancaster and his family suffered scorn and derision from their neighbours whenever they related the tale. Finally, in 1745 they summoned the most vociferous of the sceptics to the farm. On Midsummer Eve a group of twenty-six people sat and waited. Sure enough, with one hour of daylight remaining a spectral army came into view right on cue. This time the soldiers and horsemen were joined by a half-mile train of carriages, and all those present at the farm knew that it was impossible to draw carriages across Souther Fell. Once again the procession lasted for over an hour, eventually being hidden by the night.

All twenty-six witnesses signed an affidavit in the presence of magistrates, and all agreed that the vision was remarkably clear. They could easily distinguish individual shapes and colours, and the apparition was totally free from any vaporous or wavering effects. The image was so lifelike that the following morning a party climbed to the ridge to search for prints in the grass and heather. None was found. In 1785 the surviving witnesses were interviewed again, this time by a clergyman. Each of them swore that their earlier statements were true.

Nowadays it is easy to discount all this as a form of mass hallucination brought on by suggestion. But there is another possible cause. It transpires that at the time of the 1745 sighting, Bonnie Prince Charlie's army was involved in manoeuvres around the Solway Firth, to the north-west of the Cumbrian mountains. A combination of sea mists and refracted light could have formed a mirage, explaining the last of the sightings. But the earlier two remain completely baffling.

Our route continues the long traverse up the Tongue and the path can be seen stretching far into the distance, heading for Bowscale Fell. Ahead and to the left is the dramatic rugged combe formed by Bannerdale Crags. At the foot of the cliffs there used to be a lead mine where graphite was discovered – quite a rare find in the Lake District. The mine closed around 1870 but some evidence remains of it on the ground.

As the path climbs higher Blencathra appears over the top of Bannerdale Crags and then we arrive on the crest, with only a short walk to the summit of Bowscale Fell. Although this is a broad summit, the views are still rewarding. The eastern plains are seen stretching out to the Pennines. To the south and west lie Blencathra and the Skiddaw group bedecked in heather. Beyond these the north-western fells form a distant horizon. The summit cairn stands at an altitude of 2,300ft (701m), the highest point of our walk.

From here there follows a gradual descent over thick, spongy grass until Bowscale Tarn is revealed about 400ft (120m) beneath us. The way down to the tarn requires a degree of concentration, but we soon arrive on the southern shore at an altitude of 1,570ft (479m).

Roughly pear-shaped, Bowscale Tarn measures about 220yd by 150yd (200m by 140m). The maximum depth is over 50ft (15m) and the shoreline is accessible all around apart from one small section on the south-western side. No bays or promontories worthy of the name disrupt the form and there is just one small inlet stream – the tarn is fed mainly by springs. Another combe tarn, its enclosing walls face to the north where the outflow beck falls down to merge with the River Caldew. Tarn Crags form the main back wall, with the northern side of Bowscale Fell and deep moraine completing the combe.

Left: Just after an October sunrise on Bowscale Fell, looking towards Blencathra

This is a very steep enclosure, particularly on the western side where high crags almost overhang the water. Because of the steepness and northerly bearing of the surroundings, direct sunlight is limited on the surface of the tarn, and it needs a number of hot days in succession to bring the water temperature up sufficiently for comfortable swimming.

On my first visit to Bowscale Tarn I spent the last hour of daylight fishing from the western shore near the small trees. I was about to pack up when I noticed a tiny perch following my lure. After the next cast he had brought a companion, and these two perfect miniatures escorted the lure and then stayed right at my feet, looking quizzically at the strange apparition above them.

On overcast days this can be a sombre, almost forbidding place, the stuff of which legends are made. Bowscale Tarn duly provides one. The clean, green tinted waters are said to contain two immortal trout of enormous proportions. In his 'Song at the Feast of Brougham Castle' Wordsworth writes of their great wisdom and names them Adam and Eve.

The combe of Bowscale Tarn is where I first camped alone. It had been a cloudy day, with just two other visitors to the tarn after my arrival. By dusk I was left to myself in the darkening hollow, and I wondered if staying here was such a good idea. After I had pitched my tent the clouds lifted and unveiled an inky black sky studded with brilliant blue/white diamonds. From my position deep inside the combe, it seemed as if I were sitting in a massive crater where the only light that could possibly enter came down from the stars. Under their gaze the feeling of loneliness completely left me, and I spent the rest of the night outside the tent watching the slow motions of the heavens.

Our path away from this spot follows the outflow beck for a few yards, descending over the containing moraine. Mosedale opens out below as the path grows wider at the foot of the moraine, becoming a farm track which traverses the north face of Bowscale Fell in a gentle descent to Bowscale hamlet.

Roughly opposite the point where the path becomes a track, a large round house can be seen in the valley on the far side of the River Caldew. It is a dream of a place, surrounded by lawns, flowers and trees, and constantly serenaded by the river. Beyond the house Carrock Fell rises up to form the valley's northern rampart. The fell shows an impressive face from our viewpoint, with many contrasting textures and colours. There are dark and light greys in the angular shapes of rocks and slates, with various shades of green in the grasses. Bracken and heather provide purples, reds and browns leading up to the summit, where the remains of an Iron Age fort are visible. The fort was the most important part of Cumbria's defences during inter-tribal disputes before Roman domination. It is believed that the Romans removed most of the construction as it had no strategic significance for them, and could have been used by resistance groups.

Birds of prey are a common sight over Mosedale. Recently a pair of golden eagles were seen over a period of two weeks. But eagles need very specialised hunting grounds and they did not settle; even these remote mountains and valleys failed to meet their requirements. Buzzards, however are not as choosy, and I have often seen them circling the peaks above here or skimming the trees and hedges below.

After Bowscale hamlet, all that remains is a stroll along the lane back to Mungrisedale. Far reaching, open ground lies to the left, leading up to Greystoke Forest. To the right are Raven Crags, marking the eastern tip of Bowscale Fell. Along the way, Shetland ponies can usually be seen grazing by the roadside. They belong to one of Bowscale's farms.

Soon the lane enters the fields around Mungrisedale, passing a series of cottages and the church before bringing us back to our starting point.

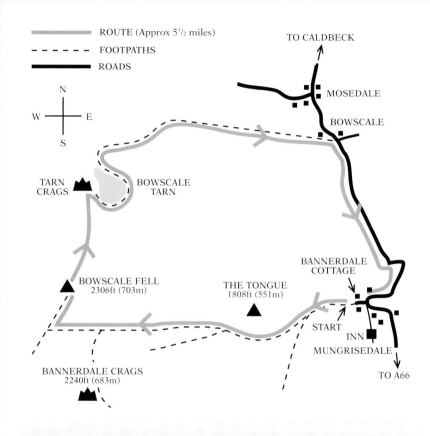

Map legend:
- ROUTE (Approx 5½ miles)
- - - - - FOOTPATHS
- ROADS

TO CALDBECK
MOSEDALE
BOWSCALE
TARN CRAGS
BOWSCALE TARN
BOWSCALE FELL 2306ft (703m)
THE TONGUE 1808ft (551m)
BANNERDALE COTTAGE
START
INN
MUNGRISEDALE
TO A66
BANNERDALE CRAGS 2240ft (683m)

ROUTE SUMMARY

MAP: OS Landranger Map 90

START: Mungrisedale, GR 362303

DISTANCE: Approximately 5½ miles (9km)

TIME: 2¼ – 2¾ hours

DIFFICULTY: Care must be taken when descending to the tarn

ROUTE DIRECTIONS

To reach the starting point take the road that goes north from the A66 to Mungrisedale. In the village the road bends sharply to the left, passes a bridge on the left, and then comes to a red telephone box and a cul-de-sac, once again on the left. There is a small parking area here.

1 You will see a sign saying 'Public Footpath Mungrisedale Common'. Follow the path past Bannerdale Cottage and through the farm buildings, onto the open fells where it widens.

2 When it reaches the foot of the facing hill, the path crosses a footbridge and then forks. Take the major path to your right. Approximately half way up to Bowscale Fell, you will see another path branching to your left; go past this and continue the ascent.

3 At the top of the rise the obvious path bears left along the crest of the ridge towards Bannerdale Crags, but do not go any further along it. At this point you must leave it. Head north-west, looking for dark patches in the grass. After a few yards you should pick up a faint track leading to a much clearer path that cuts across the way.

4 Turn right on this up to Bowscale Fell summit. If you cannot find the faint track, simply head due north from the point where you left the clear path at the top of the rise. Your northerly direction leads straight to the summit.

5 Here you will first pass a shelter, then a cairn, after which the path disappears.

6 To the north-east, on Carrock Fell, a large cairn can be seen on the skyline. Head directly towards it, descending across the grass. In misty conditions take a compass reading and head north-east. Do not rush though, for you are approaching the top of Bowscale Tarn's combe. About five minutes after leaving the summit of Bowscale Fell the tarn appears below.

7 Bear left, following the lip of the combe towards Tarn Crags.

8 Keep looking to the right into the combe and you will see the beginning of a narrow track that goes sharply to the right, and leads all the way across the southern wall of the combe. This passes the tarn before doubling back on itself, arriving at the south-eastern tip of the shore. It is not necessary to follow it all the way down, as you can cut off the track and down to the tarn wherever you feel comfortable.

9 At the tarn you will see a clear path that follows a few feet above the southern and western shores. Follow this to the outflow beck and then on down the hillside. It is a clear and comfortable path which leads down to Bowscale hamlet and the road.

10 Turn right on the road back to Mungrisedale.

CHAPTER 5

SCALES TARN
VIA
BLENCATHRA

Midday in autumn at Scales Tarn. Tarn Crags and Sharp Edge tower above the water

The story of the Lake District began in the Ordovician period around 500 million years ago when silt settled on the sea bed to form mud stones and sand stones. Later in the same period, eruptions brought lava to the surface, forming a large volcanic island. Later still, during the Silurian period, more silt and sand stones were formed beneath the sea.

About 400 million years ago, the collision of two continental plates forced the entire region upwards, forming a high mountain range. The upheaval folded and faulted the different rock types, producing the contrasting formations we see today. The original mountain range was as high as the modern Himalayas, but was reduced to its present level by millions of years of erosion.

Rocks of the Silurian period form the southern part of the Lake District. They are soft and cannot resist the effects of weathering. Evidence of this can be seen in the rounded, forested hills of the Windermere area. Harder volcanic rocks of the late Ordovician period formed the central parts of Lakeland, resulting in the high craggy fells so popular with walkers and mountaineers. This area is known as the Borrowdale Volcanics group.

The area covered in this chapter lies to the north and is composed of the oldest rocks of all, the Skiddaw group. Their content of sediment and mud rendered them susceptible to weathering, like the Windermere group, and they now present a rounded landscape of fells that reach from Derwent Water to the northern tip of the Caldbeck Fells. Here and there within the Skiddaw group, small intrusions of granite break the surface, disrupting the smooth flow of the hills. It is largely due to these intrusions that Blencathra mountain (also known as Saddleback) today presents such a contrasting picture, with smooth slopes on the northern side and rough crags on the southern.

Of all the major Lakeland peaks, Blencathra stands most alone.

The A66 road from Keswick to Penrith passes through a wide open valley at the foot of the mountain, and motorists are treated to the awesome spectacle of a giant rising straight out of the fields. Five long ridges radiate from the southern side, topped by twin peaks that join in the shape of a saddle.

The isolated positions of Blencathra and its neighbour Skiddaw provide what I believe are the finest views in Lakeland. Also, it is these two which are most easily visible from a distance. The fells of the Skiddaw group are largely heather-clad, and this rich carpet seems to retain its colour longer than in other places. I have seen the whole range blazing like fire during autumn sunsets.

THE WALK

Our objective on this walk is Scales Tarn, set high in one of Blencathra's combes. Along the way we pass over the full length of this, my favourite mountain. Throughout the chapter I will use the name Blencathra rather than Saddleback in keeping with other places in the area which retain their Celtic names. The walking time is approximately three and a half hours, but there is so much to see and enjoy that it is likely you will spend five or six hours on the journey. The initial ascent up Blease Fell is a long one, but after that the path is comfortable.

The route begins above Threlkeld village at a parking area beside the Blencathra Centre. This is a modern accommodation complex operated by the National Park Authority, and offers cottages for rent and hostel places. It is also the clearing house for other similar establishments throughout the Lake District. For details ring 017687 79601.

On leaving the centre the way leads up through masses of bracken and a cropped, grassy path. It heads towards Knowe Crags

on Blease Fell, which forms the western rampart of Blencathra. Views open out immediately towards the left and behind, gradually expanding to include Derwent Water, Keswick and the western fells. Due south lies Clough Head and beyond that Helvellyn. The wide valley containing the A66 lies directly below.

The going is steep, gaining height rapidly. Blease Fell falls away on the left into the gorge of Glenderaterra Beck, after which the land climbs steeply up Longscale Fell. Next along the same line of sight come the heather covered slopes of Lower Man and Skiddaw.

A series of false summits dash any hopes of a quick ascent, as Thirlmere enters the view below Helvellyn. It is between fifty minutes and an hour of hard work, but is rewarded by our arrival at Knowe Crags. Now is the time to rest and enjoy a 360 degree panorama that cannot be equalled. The breathtaking view contains far too much to itemise fully, but starting from the south, and moving clockwise, the major points are as follows.

Across the valley lie Helvellyn and Thirlmere among the central fells. Then come the main bulk of the western fells, so colourful in autumn. Derwent Water and Keswick are followed by the Irish Sea and the northern tip of the Isle of Man. Then we see masses of heather on Skiddaw and its companion fells, incorporating the broad sweep of Skiddaw Forest. The eye passes on to the Solway Firth and beyond to southern Scotland. The Caldbeck Fells come next, followed by wide plains around and beyond Penrith. The distant Pennines are bisected by Blencathra's highest peaks and their precipitous, jagged ridges. Finally there are the eastern fells with the full array of High Street's range. In all this I find that the most impressive aspect is of the sheer, rocky cliffs right at our feet. As they fall down to the valley, they offer a stark contrast to the pastel shades and uniform shapes of the fields and distant plains.

The group of mountains to which Blencathra belongs is rich in

Lakeland folklore and history. In past centuries, large bonfires were built on high ground to act as a chain of beacons linking the whole country. On Skiddaw such a beacon was used to pass news of national events such as the sighting of the Spanish Armada, and as advance warning of local incursions by raiders from the north or the sea. More recently, similar fires have been lit during anniversaries and celebrations.

There has been a strong tradition of hunting in the area, ever since Norse settlers christened Skiddaw (the 'Archer's Hill'). Deep within the fells at the feet of Skiddaw Forest, a lone building can be found alongside the Cumbria Way. This is Skiddaw House, built to accommodate the gamekeepers of the bountiful grouse hills. Nowadays, despite the remote location, it is used as a Youth Hostel.

The area's best-known hunting connection is with England's legendary fox hunter, John Peel. Although the exact date is unknown, he was born at Caldbeck in the 1770s. He married while still very young and quickly settled down to develop the land endowed to him by his marriage. This gave him the opportunity to build a sizeable pack of hounds, and a string of horses. For the next fifty years his prowess as a huntsman made him famous. His friend John Graves wrote a song about him, describing his great chases around the fells 'in his coat so grey.' This refers to the coats made from Herdwick wool which favoured by Cumbrian huntsmen of the era. The scarlet coats of modern times have spread from the south. The song was published nationally and John Peel has been a celebrated figure ever since. The present Blencathra Fox Hounds still hunt over land which he owned.

Now our route leaves the first of Blencathra's ridges on Knowe Crags and climbs gradually up to the top of the second ridge, Gategill Fell. This marks the beginning of the saddle shape on the highest section of the mountain. Spare a moment here to consider the fact that with 500 million years of history beneath your feet, you are standing on the oldest surface rock in Europe.

Tewet Tarn on Low Rigg can be seen on the far side of the valley, about 2,150ft (650m) below us. One day I watched two men take off on their hang-gliders from the pinnacle of Gategill Fell. Effortlessly, they cruised down from the heights, crossing over the valley and landing on the tarn's shore. It was a demonstration that left me awestruck and, I admit, more than a touch envious.

From here we move across the saddle, arriving at Blencathra's summit above Hall's Fell Ridge, the third in the series of ridges. At 2,847ft (868m) this is only ranked fourteenth highest in Lakeland, something which you will find hard to believe as you gaze out from it. The patchwork effect of the north-eastern plains is much more noticeable now, and all around we still have the views I mentioned earlier.

A large cross made from white, crystalline rock is set into the ground a few yards north of this point, on the plateau that leads to Atkinson Pike. It is a monument to a former gamekeeper of Skiddaw House, who was killed in World War II, and was erected by a friend of his, a fell runner who carried the stones up from the valley, sometimes making more than one trip in the same day. Another smaller cross lies nearby. It is not known who built it, or why, but it is believed to have been constructed from stones taken from the earlier cross.

At this point, there is a choice of paths down to Scales Tarn. It is possible to continue along the summit path and reach the tarn via Sharp Edge. But even in perfect conditions this descent can cause problems. It is always more difficult to go down mountain ridges than it is to climb them, and this one is the most difficult in Lakeland. Crossing the edge itself is not the main problem, as there is a path to the left of the edge proper. The real danger is the buttresses and rock walls before you reach the edge. Exciting as it is, I advise you not to

Right: Keswick, Derwent Water and the Derwent Fells. Viewed from the route over Knowe Crags on a late autumn morning

go this way unless you are a confident, experienced fell walker (and adept climber). In strong winds or slippery conditions, do not even think about it.

The easier route leads onto the fourth ridge, Doddick Fell. From here Scales Tarn is revealed below to the left, while the fifth and final ridge of Blencathra lies ahead in the form of Scales Fell. A sixth ridge sweeps down beyond Scales Tarn from the heights of Bannerdale Crags. Our path leads into the deep combe of the tarn, shadowed by high crags.

Much has been written and said about Scales Tarn. Victorian visitors described the combe as wild and inhospitable. Like Blea Water above Mardale, Scales was believed to be bottomless and to fill the crater of an extinct volcano – a false impression, but understandable when one sees the scree covered walls that fall steeply into the water. Tarn Crags forms the main back wall, tapering out on the jagged teeth of Sharp Edge.

The maximum depth is over 25ft (8m) and the water is held in place by moraine deposited by glacial action. As with all other tarns, the true architect of the hollow was ice. Roughly circular in shape, it measures approximately 175yd by 125yd (160m by 110m), and lies at an altitude of 2,000ft (610m). There does not appear to be any permanent inlet stream, and the only outflow flows down to join the River Glenderamackin.

Early accounts often describe the water as being very dark, but that depends on the angle from which it is viewed. From the outflow side it reflects the towering walls, and is of course dark. But from the shore beneath Tarn Crags looking to the open sky, the water assumes a beautiful pale blue hue, and is very welcoming on a hot day. Despite the steep walls, the shoreline is easily accessible all around. I do not know of any fish here, but I have seen telltale ripples on the surface, probably of small trout. Near the outflow stream on the northern side of the tarn is the best place for camping.

One of the classic combe tarns, its dramatic environment has led to some romantic tales. Sir Walter Scott wrote that the sun never shines on Scales Tarn, but I can assure you that it does. It has also been said that when viewed from above the back walls, certain tarns reflect the stars even in daylight, and that Scales is a good example. I believe that in exceptional conditions of light and shade during winter, this effect is indeed possible, but I know of no contemporary witnesses.

On leaving, the path descends 200ft (60m) beside Scales Beck, and then follows the contour of Scales Fell en route back to Threlkeld. The River Glenderamackin lies beneath us as we move parallel with Bannerdale Crags down a long valley. The course of the river then curves round to the north towards Mungrisedale and our path bends to the right, in the opposite direction. It passes along a narrow ledge in the steep hillside, and an old railway viaduct which used to carry the Penrith/Keswick line can be seen in the valley below. The descent becomes steeper and soon we are back in the main valley almost at road level. There still remains a lengthy walk back to the Blencathra Centre but this is enlivened by a series of streams and gorges.

Around the first stream some chain handrails have been fixed to the walls of the gully to help walkers, a very thoughtful innovation. A line of sight up this gully between Doddick and Scales Fells reveals Tarn Crags towering above us. Then comes a second gully and stream between Doddick and Hall's Fells from which we can see Sharp Edge beyond the heather covered gorge.

At the third gully between Gategill and Hall's Fells, Threlkeld village can be seen to the left. A little further on we pass through the fourth and final gully stream between Gategill and Blease Fells. Keswick reappears ahead of us and soon we make a short descent to the lane that leads back to the Blencathra Centre.

Left: Looking towards the western fells from Blencathra
on a late summer evening

ROUTE DIRECTIONS

1 At the parking area behind the Blencathra Centre, a sign marked 'Public Footpath' points up the slope towards a grass path. Take this path through the ferns.

2 Very soon you will come to a spot where a path branches left. Take this left branch and from there the way is clear all the way to the top of Knowe Crags.

3 At the top follow the track along the summit cliffs. This leads over the first of the saddle peaks and then onto the top of Hall's Fell Ridge.

4 Go past the path that leads down Hall's Fell and you come to a choice of routes. Continuing along the highest path to the left leads to Sharp Edge, an extremely difficult descent. Eventually this path goes down to Scales Tarn. The more sensible route is to the right at this point. This leads down Doddick Fell.

5 As you descend keep looking over to your left into the combe of Scales Tarn. After walking about 100yd (90m) down the path, you will see another path that goes left and down to the tarn. It is not marked on Ordnance Survey maps but on the ground it is very clear. Take it.

6 At the tarn cross the outflow beck and then turn right on the path beside the stream.

7 Recross the beck a little further down where the path forks. Our route is the major one that curves to the right following the contour of the hillside.

8 Walk along the hillside on this path and when you come to a branch leading to the right, follow it.

9 After this go straight across a cross-path, heading downwards. The path curves to the west around the end of Scales Fell and then descends to the valley.

10 Now almost down at road level, stay on the main path and ignore any forks to the left that lead to the road. A series of four gully streams cut across the way.

11 Having crossed the fourth stream, follow the permissive footpath sign up a short steep rise to a stile.

12 Immediately after the stile the path appears to go to the right, up the fell side. Bear to the left alongside the wall. After a few paces the path becomes obvious and then descends to a lane.

13 Turn right on the lane back to the Blencathra Centre.

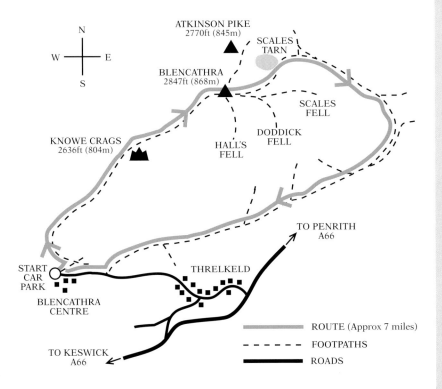

ROUTE SUMMARY

MAP: OS Outdoor Leisure Map 5

START: Blencathra Centre, GR 302256

DISTANCE: Approximately 7 miles (11km)

TIME: 3$\frac{1}{2}$ – 4 hours

DIFFICULTY: High level route, steep ascent

In the north-western corner of the Lake District, closely packed mountains begin to spread where long finger valleys reach into the National Park from the lowlands. Fleetwith Pike at the head of Buttermere marks the tip of such a valley, the Vale of Lorton. From its head the course of the vale snakes through Buttermere then Crummock Water before continuing north to Cockermouth. At the northern reaches of Crummock Water a lesser valley branches to the left, passing through a final mountain gateway to the lowlands and the perimeter of the National Park. In that gateway lies Loweswater, a beautiful and peaceful lake.

Located far from the main tourist routes, Loweswater is seldom seen by any but true Lake District connoisseurs and local visitors from the coastal areas. The lake and adjacent woodland are owned by the National Trust, which puts great effort into conserving the area while keeping it open to the public.

Carling Knott and Black Crag stand to the south-west of the lake, with a niche between which holds High Nook Tarn. I feel it is only fair to say at this juncture that those who regard the tarn as the main aim of their walk might be disappointed by High Nook. It is a very small water and only a hopeless romantic could describe it as beautiful. However, it is so perfectly situated on a superb route that it demands inclusion. It lies practically half way along a walk that can be enjoyed by all categories of walkers. Even beginners will have no problems in completing a circuit that covers approximately 5½ miles (9km), and presents an unbeatable showcase of this wonderful area. Two and a half hours walking time should be sufficient.

The route begins close to Loweswater's northern tip, where it leaves the road and crosses over a number of fields. The lake is to the left, providing a foreground for the heather covered slopes of Melbreak, Whiteless Pike and Grasmoor. Beyond Loweswater's

CHAPTER 6

HIGH NOOK TARN
LOWESWATER

High Nook Tarn and the Vale of Lorton, viewed from Black Crag in autumn

wooded western shore the high peaks around Buttermere and Ennerdale can be seen in the distance.

We begin to move away from the lake, gaining height almost imperceptibly as the route follows a lane and then passes by a number of cottages and farm buildings. The ascent continues through fields and leafy tracks, then comes out onto open moorland. Soon the path begins to curve back towards Loweswater, still climbing gently. At this point our route is on the very border of the National Park. Behind us lies a vast patchwork plain that stretches to the sea, and the whole Lake District stands before us as we head towards the mountains.

The forward vista expands to include Crummock Water and then Loweswater re-enters the picture. The farm track under foot gives way to a very comfortable grassy path through a bracken-covered slope. As we continue, the craggy peaks around Crummock Water grow in stature and then the view opens out completely. It comes as a great surprise to realise how much height we have gained. Suddenly from surroundings of moorland and plains the path has carried us above a landscape of forest, mountains and lakes that would grace a Canadian tourist brochure.

This perfectly situated path continues above the tree line about half way up the eastern slope of Burnbank Fell. Another slight rise takes us to the highest point of the tree line and the best views of the day. The woods fall steeply to Loweswater beneath us while the colourful mountain range east and north of Crummock Water domi-

Above: Loweswater and Holme Wood from Burnbank Fell on a glorious autumn afternoon. Whiteside and Grasmoor in the clouds

nates the skyline. Deciduous woodland occupies the lake shore and lower slopes, rising into commercial pine woods immediately in front of us. Buzzards and peregrine falcons wheel above the treetops that rustle with nervous red squirrels.

Around the northern and southern extremities of the lake, arable land lends a softer touch to a picture that is an absolute credit to the National Trust. I cannot think of another path in the Lake District that offers such a rewarding view and yet asks for so little effort. It serves as an ideal introduction for newcomers and will surely spur them on to more demanding routes.

We continue to skirt the crest of the woods as our path begins to descend. Soon the woods' southern boundary falls sharply away down the fellside and High Nook Tarn lies ahead and beneath us in its sheltered mountain hollow. The main route veers east and then north-east slightly before the tarn. A detour of only a few paces leads to the north-western corner of the shore, close by the outflow.

Set apart as it is from a track that could not be described as 'beaten', High Nook Tarn rests quietly in its shelf between the slopes. Out of sight on the surrounding fells, there is evidence that the tarn might have had a busier past. The remains of various dwellings, earth works and tumuli are dotted around the grassy tops and an old pack-horse track used to pass close by. Now the tarn is very much alone. Set to the east of the shelf it faces north and is by-passed on the western side by High Nook Beck. This stream issues from high above on Gavel Fell and then continues through the shelf, collecting the tarn's outflow in its passage. The surroundings on three sides are high, but do not fall steeply into the hollow. Instead, they have a gentler, rolling character, in keeping with the spongy shoreline of the tarn and the long grasses of the shelf.

The tarn measures 90yd by 70yd (80m by 65m) and is roughly square. Marshy ground around part of it prevents a comfortable ap-

proach to the water, which has a maximum depth of 6ft (1.8m), and lies at an altitude of 720ft (219m). Tiny islands protrude above the surface, which remains undisturbed by anything other than newts and reeds. A small deposit of moraine cradles the tarn, aided by a line of stones and earth along the western rim.

High Nook Tarn offers a chance to cool off during hot weather, and children will enjoy its mainly shallow water. For walkers who seek solitude without having to travel far this is an excellent spot.

An easy descent follows back to Loweswater. The path heads directly towards the Vale of Lorton and an array of purple-clad peaks seen in the far reaches of the valley. High Nook Beck falls through a deep gully to our left and then the path re-enters farmland and trees.

After crossing the fields and passing along the perimeter of a long, narrow copse, our route comes to a gate, which leads straight onto Watergate Farm's lawn! I was completely mystified by this on my first visit as there did not appear to be any other direction in which to go. Gingerly stepping across the grass, I adopted my most apologetic expression and then saw the route resume its course beyond the cottages. So, unlikely as it seems, the route really does go straight across the clipped grass.

Immediately afterwards, we enter the woods close by the lake's shore. This is a delightful way to re-enter the valley, passing through mixed woodland with a series of tiny beaches on the shore just a matter of a few feet away from us. There is an unlimited selection of picnic spots here. The trees are well spaced and the ground between them is flat and grassy.

Various paths run through the full length of the woods, but the one closest to the shore is the most enjoyable, listening to gently lapping water and rustling trees. Then our path rejoins the main track which leads back to the lane. From here all that remains is a short walk across the fields once more to return to our starting point.

ROUTE DIRECTIONS

A public telephone box stands by the roadside a little to the north of Loweswater. Here, you will find a small parking area and a gate marked 'Public Footpath'.

1 Go through the gate and cross the field to a stile.

2 Once over the stile cross the next field, passing over some wet ground on a wooden walkway. This leads to another stile, then another walkway, arriving at a gate beside a lane.

3 Turn left and follow the lane until you reach a sign marked 'Public Bridleway Fangs Brow' a few yards from the farm houses of Hudson Place at the top of the lane.

4 Turn right at the sign through a gate and stile.

5 Where the path becomes unclear follow the wall on your left.

6 Turn right at the next gate, after which the path leads to another gate. Through this, the path is unclear once more but can just be discerned bearing slightly to the left and uphill.

7 Next comes a gap in a wall and then the path leads across a field heading to the left (west) of Jenkinson Place Cottages.

8 Before you reach the cottages, a stile leads onto a tarmac lane. Indicators on both sides of the stile point in the wrong direction, but the obvious way is along the lane to the right.

9 Where the lane forks bear left, following a blue direction marker. Another gate follows, after which the path leads out onto moorland.

10 Follow the wall on your left, and go past the first gate you see.

11 Eventually you will arrive at a wall stile. Cross the stile and turn left on the bridle-way.

12 After the next stile the bridleway forks. Go left .

13 The path leads above Holme Wood, moving parallel to the lake. The route remains clear all the way to a footbridge close to High Nook Tarn.

14 Cross the footbridge and then turn right at the cross-path. This leads to the tarn.

15 Return to the cross-path and turn sharp right on a wide grassy track. This leads to a gate after which comes the descent to High Nook Farm.

16 Pass through the farm buildings and over a bridge.

17 You will see a wall stile on your left and a sign saying 'National Trust. Permitted footpath to Watergate and Loweswater'. Although unclear, this path leads across a field and heads straight for a stile on the opposite side. If in doubt, move across the field, keeping a copse of trees about 30yds (25m) to your left and eventually you will see the stile ahead.

18 Once over the stile, follow the path alongside the fence on your right.

19 Cross the next stile and then the path follows the right hand boundary of a long copse, with a fence on your right, arriving at the gate to Watergate Farm.

20 Here the path disappears, but carry on over the grass to the lakeside path.

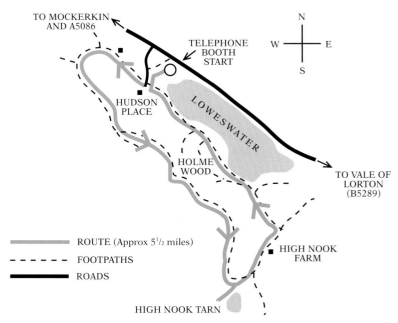

ROUTE (Approx 5½ miles) — — — FOOTPATHS ROADS

21 Turn left onto this path immediately after Watergate.

22 Inside the woods, follow the sign for 'Holme Wood Bothy'. To follow the lake shore take the branch to the right wherever the path forks.

23 Where the lakeside path rejoins the main path through the woods, turn right and return to Hudson Place.

24 Go down the lane and turn right through the fields back to your starting point.

ROUTE SUMMARY

MAP:	OS Outdoor Leisure Map 4
START:	Telephone box near Waterend, Loweswater, GR 117224
DISTANCE:	Approximately 5½ miles (9km)
TIME:	2¼ – 2¾ hours
DIFFICULTY:	None

Only Wast Water's surroundings can compare to those of Buttermere at the head of the Vale of Lorton. Here, the compact valley is sheltered by some of Lakeland's best-loved peaks. Beyond Buttermere's southern shore, the distinctive pinnacle of Fleetwith Pike stands at the valley's south-eastern gateway, towering above the road from Honister Pass. Robinson and High Snock Rigg fall steeply to the lake's western shore, but it is on the eastern side that the most eminent names are found. Haystacks, High Crag, High Stile, Red Pike and a series of high ridges and cols form an unbroken chain which presents one of the finest skylines in the National Park. This is our route to three tarns. The scenic splendour continues through the open mouth of the valley in the north-west, where only a narrow strip of land separates Buttermere from Crummock Water, itself flanked by yet more high peaks.

Buttermere village lies adjacent to the delta between the lakes, at the point where a minor road comes down from the easterly Derwent Fells. This tiny settlement became a focus of national interest when it was the setting for a classical tale of beauty and beastliness. In the late eighteenth century, an article was published describing the unparalleled loveliness of Mary Robinson, a local innkeeper's daughter. Unfortunately, the story caught the attention of one John Hatfield, a notorious fraud and bigamist. Posing as an aristocrat, he successfully wooed Mary and the pair were married. However, the wedding notices alerted his creditors, who brought about his arrest and trial. When he was hanged in 1803 Mary was pregnant, but had no difficulty in finding another husband. A recent novel by Melvyn Bragg is based upon these events.

Nowadays, Buttermere has another 'beast' – an enormous sheep named Lucy, which takes great delight in robbing tourists of anything edible. She will enter the village café to see if there is anything of interest. If not, she returns to her favourite pastime of worrying dogs.

CHAPTER 7

BLEABERRY, INNOMINATE & BLACKBECK TARNS

The last light of an October day fades above Innominate Tarn and Wainwright's ashes

into view to our rear. The mountainous vista grows ever wider and far reaching, with Whitless Pike and Grasmoor the pick of the closer peaks, dominating Crummock Water's far shore.

We approach Sourmilk Gill's deep, heather-covered ravine and then follow it up onto the shelf that contains Bleaberry Tarn. As yet the tarn itself remains unseen, lying deep in the combe beneath the towering wall of Chapel Crags. The path leads through rocks, grass and heather toward a slight mound of moraine, then arrives at the tarn's outflow, 1,620ft (494m) above sea level.

Buttermere Lake itself cannot be seen from the tarn, as it is hidden by the far lip of the combe. Long encircling arms shelter the hollow, which is formed on the south-eastern side by High Stile. The back wall of Chapel Crags curves round to Red Pike, which leads in turn to the north-western arm formed by The Saddle.

A small shallow combe lies above the tarn on High Stile's facing slope, and this was once the site of another tarn, which dried up. Bleaberry Tarn itself is not in any danger of a similar fate; its clear water reaches a depth of about 20ft (6m). It measures approximately 170yd (150m) by 100yd (90m) and is accessible all around, save for one small, marshy section beneath Red Pike.

There are many good camping locations in the combe for those who wish to spend more time here, and perhaps try their luck at catching a brown trout. I am told by Steven Richardson of the Fish Hotel that Bleaberry's fish have a fondness for bread, and can grow to respectable sizes.

A solitary inlet stream comes down from Red Pike, a mountain renowned for breathtaking scenery. Our route heads for the summit. On the ascent, the derivation of Red Pike's name becomes apparent in the rich colour of the earth, tinted by a high content of iron stone. The view constantly acquires more peaks and landmarks until our path reaches the summit shelter and cairns at an altitude of 2,477ft

Our route to the peaks and tarns above Buttermere covers a distance of about 8½ miles (13.5km). Walking time is almost five hours, so at least six should be allowed. This is a very high-level route with steep climbs and descents, and should only be attempted by experienced walkers.

Beginning at the Fish Hotel, our path passes through fields of grazing cattle and sheep, heading towards the lake and the forested slopes of Red Pike and High Stile. The senses are drawn to Sourmilk Gill as it falls through the trees for hundreds of feet, and seems to fill the valley with sound.

After passing the lake's north-western tip, the route climbs steeply on a stone-built path through trees. Above the tree line, the full length of Buttermere is revealed and Crummock Water comes

Above: (from the right) Red Pike, High Stile, High Crag, Haystacks and Fleetwith Pike's lower slopes; all the peaks of the route

(755m). Here, the outlook simply explodes into a 360 degree panorama which contains every imaginable feature of mountain country. Looking first to the north, and then in a clockwise direction, the majestic form of Grasmoor, Whitless Pike and their companion fells stand high above Crummock Water's shining surface. Beyond Buttermere, Newlands Valley heads toward Derwent Water, Keswick, Skiddaw, Blencathra and the distant Pennines. Much nearer, Robinson, Hindscarth and Dale Head give way to the sharp face of Fleetwith Pike, with a background formed by the Helvellyn range and the Langdale Pikes. High Stile lies close at hand, then the Scafells, Pillar

Above: Bleaberry Tarn and Red Pike from High Stile, with Crummock Water leading on to the Vale of Lorton

buttresses and sheer cliffs. On gaining the summit, our route reaches its highest point, at an altitude of 2,647ft (807m). The Gables come into view, with the Scafells and Pillar dominating the scene to the south.

On the narrow col between High Stile and High Crag, the path passes very close to buttresses and cliffs on Eagle and Comb Crags, an area favoured by rock climbers. A very steep path zigzags down from High Crag, overlooking Haystacks and Scarth Gap. The path on which we will eventually return to the valley can be seen on Fleetwith Pike, hundreds of feet below. At the bottom of the descent, a glance behind you shows High Crag's pointed profile, with its summit a surprising distance above. Then we cross Seat and descend into Scarth Gap, after which a steep scramble leads into innumerable knolls and outcrops on the summit plateau of Haystacks.

The path threads its way through and over these obstacles to reveal Innominate Tarn at an altitude of 1,750ft (533m). This delightful water rests among rock outcrops which open on the north-western shore into grass and marsh. Heather abounds among the multicoloured rocks and grasses here, contrasting with the darker summits of the encircling peaks. These peer into Haystacks's plateau, which has a distinctly fortress-like character emphasised by its outer ring of knolls and crags. It is a particularly restful spot, with many camping locations among the knolls. The tarn is roughly circular in shape, with a diameter of approximately 100yd (90m). Fed by marshy ground to the north-west, the water reaches a maximum depth of about 7ft (2m). Because of its position near the summit, the tarn's surface mirrors the sky: a bright blue gem set in purples, reds, greys, greens and yellows. Access to the water is easiest on the north-eastern side, where the path comes down to the shore, and the first few paces into the tarn can be taken in relative comfort. The celebrated Lakeland commentator Alfred Wainwright loved this place above all others.

and the other Red Pike (near Wast Water) complete the rugged section of the panorama. Ennerdale Forest and Lake are to the east, where the outlook changes completely. The softer, rolling aspect of Little Dodd, Starling Dodd and Great Borne are the natural extension of the mountain chain. They lead to, and complement, a wide angle of the view which is composed of Mellbreak, Loweswater, the coastal plains, the Solway Firth and a vast expanse of sea. The finishing touches to this achingly beautiful picture are provided by the hills of southern Scotland.

The route continues along the crest of Bleaberry Tarn's combe, heading toward High Stile's rocky summit. Views of the tarn and its background of mountains open and close between clefts in precipitous

Above: Blackbeck Tarn, looking towards Buttermere's northern shore and Crummock Water

A golden summer sunset above Buttermere, Crummock Water and distant Loweswater. Viewed from Fleetwith Pike

His ashes are scattered around Innominate Tarn, in the inner sanctum of the mountain.

After paying our respects, we take the path down to where it skirts sheer cliffs, slightly below the summit of Haystacks. The valley opens out beneath us, seen through impressive rock buttresses, and the sounds of Black Beck's waterfalls act as a reminder that the finest tarn on the route is yet to come.

At the beck, a path goes upstream through a cleft in the mountainside, revealing Blackbeck Tarn surprisingly close to the precipitous falls. At an altitude of 1,550ft (472m), this tarn's improbable position above cliffs offers wonderful views over Buttermere and Crummock Water. The outflow crashes down to the valley, joining Warnscale Beck on its journey to the lake. Through the cleft of the outflow, the tops of High Stile and High Crag can be seen beyond the rocky slope of Haystacks.

The tarn is fed by streams at the southern end, opposite the outflow. They come in through the only flat, marshy section of the surrounding area. Elsewhere the tarn has a rocky perimeter, with some outcrops on the western side which fall steeply into the water. Beyond the south-eastern shore, the land rises gradually up to Brandreth, with Great Gable dominating the skyline a little further to the south. This is another bright and colourful location, liberally decorated with heather, grasses and knolls. Those who seek it out are usually left to explore in peace, despite the close proximity of the mountain path. This is because no other route passes by the shore, and most walkers continue along the mountain ridge, unaware of the treasure so close at hand.

The tarn is roughly pear-shaped, and measures approximately 220yd (200m) from north to south, and 100yd (90m) across before it tapers toward the outflow. Owing to its mountain top position, there is not a deep hollow or combe to contain the water, which has a maximum depth of less than 10ft (3m). However, that is more than sufficient for comfortable swimming, and adequate protection for the numerous brown trout.

Having reached this point, there is no further climbing on the route. All that remains is the descent to Buttermere, and a stroll back to the village along the lake shore. Blackbeck Tarn is therefore the logical camping spot on the journey. For those who stay, further exploration of the surroundings will reveal many delightful viewpoints, particularly on the western side of the mountain overlooking Ennerdale Forest.

On the descent from the tarn, the path crosses a deep ravine, resplendent with waterfalls. As it curves around Fleetwith Pike en route to Buttermere, the serrated crags of Haystacks tower above us, appearing deceptively high. From this vantage point, there seems to be little difference between their altitude and that of High Crag, but think back to where the route passed over them, and you will realise that the effect is an illusion.

Down in the valley, the path skirts Fleetwith Pike's lower slopes, where a white cross looks out over the lake. This is a memorial to a young servant girl named Fanny Mercer, who fell to her death there in 1887.

We follow the road for a short distance, then step onto the lake shore. A permissive path runs the full length of the eastern side, with all the mighty peaks of our route facing us across the water. It is an idyllic ending to one of the most rewarding walks in Lakeland, with copses of trees shading us along the way. On one section of about 50yd (45m), our path passes through a tunnel blasted into the rock, then emerges to lead through farm houses, returning eventually to the Fish Hotel.

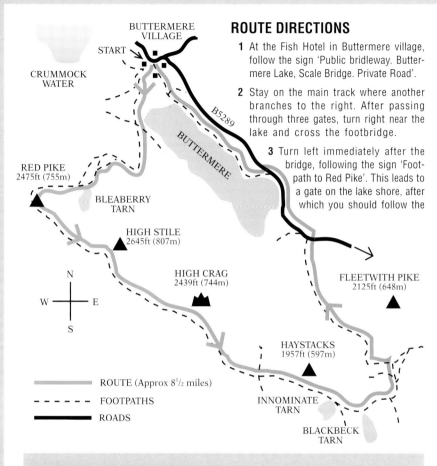

CRUMMOCK
WATER

BUTTERMERE
VILLAGE

START

BUTTERMERE

B5289

RED PIKE
2475ft (755m)

BLEABERRY
TARN

HIGH STILE
2645ft (807m)

N
W E
S

HIGH CRAG
2439ft (744m)

FLEETWITH PIKE
2125ft (648m)

HAYSTACKS
1957ft (597m)

INNOMINATE
TARN

BLACKBECK
TARN

ROUTE (Approx 8½ miles)
FOOTPATHS
ROADS

ROUTE SUMMARY

MAP: OS Outdoor Leisure Map 4

START: Fish Hotel, Buttermere, GR 174169

DISTANCE: Approximately 8½ miles (13.5km)

TIME: 5 – 6 hours

DIFFICULTY: High-level, arduous walk

ROUTE DIRECTIONS

1 At the Fish Hotel in Buttermere village, follow the sign 'Public bridleway. Buttermere Lake, Scale Bridge. Private Road'.

2 Stay on the main track where another branches to the right. After passing through three gates, turn right near the lake and cross the footbridge.

3 Turn left immediately after the bridge, following the sign 'Footpath to Red Pike'. This leads to a gate on the lake shore, after which you should follow the path that turns sharply to the right, signposted 'Red Pike'.

4 Bear right where the path forks, and then the route is clear up to Sourmilk Gill. Stay on your present side of the stream and follow the path up to Bleaberrry Tarn.

5 At the tarn, cross the outflow onto the path up Red Pike.

6 Approaching the summit, the path forks twice. All paths lead to the summit, but you might find it more comfortable to go right at the first, minor fork, and then left at the major one.

7 From the summit, follow the series of cairns along the crest of Bleaberry Tarn's combe up to High Stile.

8 Here, the main pathway is marked by a line of cairns that branch along the high spur of the mountain, leading to your left (north-east). Our route bears to the right (in effect straight on) at this point, marked by other cairns.

9 Continue along the ridge-top in a south-easterly direction to High Crag. From there, a steep descent leads onto Seat and then down to Scarth Gap on a stone inlaid path.

10 Where the path peters out on Scarth Gap, turn right on the grassy path marked by small cairns.

11 Where the main track that links Ennerdale with Buttermere cuts across your way, carry on over it to Haystacks.

12 On the steep scramble to the summit, watch for a series of small cairns on top of boulders. When you see the highest one (with an iron fence post in it), bear to the right and Innominate Tarn appears ahead of you.

13 On the descent to the tarn, bear left where the path forks for the most comfortable access to the shore.

14 The path skirts Innominate Tarn's northern shore and then descends towards the mountainside. Stay on the main path where a lesser one branches to the right.

15 On arriving at a stream, turn right (up-stream) to Blackbeck Tarn.

16 To leave the tarn, return to the stream and the main path. Cross the stream, and continue along the ridge on the clear path where minor paths branch off it.

17 Two paths join from the right, after which a large cairn marks the point where the main path forks. Go left here, down the mountainside.

18 The path leads into a gorge and approaches the bridleway that runs on the opposite side of the gorge. At the closest point to the bridleway, a faint path branches across the gorge and stream, then climbs a few paces onto the bridleway. This leads all the way down to the Buttermere Road.

19 Turn left at the road, and stay on it until it reaches the lake.

20 Follow around the southern shore until the road curves to the left on the eastern side. Here, the landowner allows public access to a path that drops down onto the shore, signposted 'Buttermere via lake shore path'.

21 Follow the lake-shore path to where it leaves the lake and comes to a gate. Turn left through the gate, among the farm buildings and back to the road.

22 Turn left on the road, and then left again at the Bridge Hotel to return to the Fish Hotel.

CHAPTER 8

BORROWDALE

The fairest of all Lakeland valleys, Borrowdale extends southwards from Keswick, through Derwent Water with its sylvan shores, and on into the heart of the mountains. Richly endowed with all the charms of the Lake District, there is everything here from high crags to a crystal clear river with deciduous woodlands, green pastures and the lake. Dotted around the fields are cottages and farms, and in Rosthwaite and Grange, Borrowdale possesses two of the prettiest hamlets one could ever wish to see.

Springtime is especially enchanting here. Legend has it that many years ago the locals enjoyed the season so much that they resolved to make it last for ever. The plan was to build a wall to trap a cuckoo – the herald of spring. Of course the cuckoo escaped, but for many generations the excuse was handed down that the wall simply hadn't been built high enough!

Borrowdale holds so many delights that many visitors fail to penetrate any further into the valley than Derwent Water, which has various points of its shoreline linked to Keswick by a regular launch service. This lake and nearby Bassenthwaite Lake are the only remaining sites in Britain where vendace fish survive. Highly prized in Scandinavia, where the fish oil is used medicinally, vendace need clean water and rich plankton on which to feed. They are very rarely seen.

Formerly an area of forest and marshes, Borrowdale remained truly wild whilst many parts of Lakeland were being inhabited. It was constantly flooded and many of today's pastures were once the sites of various small lakes. The Romans were the first to make use of it, quarrying for slate. Settlers who remained after the Romans'

Left: A bright summer morning at Taylorgill Force, viewed from Base Brown's lower slopes

Right: Derwent Water, gateway to Borrowdale. Viewed from Surprise View on the road to Watendlath at the close of day

departure were forced out by marauding Scots and Angles, and had to build forts in the hills to protect themselves. Some scattered remnants of one fort can be seen on Castle Crag on the western slopes of the valley.

It wasn't until the tenth century that the land was properly cultivated by Norsemen, who had strong traditions of farming. British survivors were accepted among them and together they began to clear the overgrowth, creating fields. For the next 500 years the only livelihood was sheep and dairy farming. The arrival of the monks from Fountains Abbey and Furness during this period had the greatest impact, and most of the present valley was drained and protected from further floods by them.

Then came the limited introduction of lead and copper mining, which left little to show for its existence. The main industrialisation commenced in the eighteenth century at Honister Pass. This is the only other modern entry or exit from Borrowdale; the road runs over it westwards into Buttermere. Slate quarries were opened at the very head of the pass and became successful, reaching a peak in the 1880s, when over 100 men were employed. The site is now occupied in part by a youth hostel.

Tourism began to take off in the nineteenth century, when the small inns and farmsteads became the fine hotels and guest houses we see now. Today, most of the dales folk are occupied in the catering trade, and many of the farms supplement their incomes by offering accommodation and refreshments. Seathwaite, at the southern end of the valley beneath the mountains, is the site of a thriving fish farm. In recent times there has been virtually no unemployment in Borrowdale.

During the 1960s this area became very popular with hippies. So many settled in and around one of the quarry caves, that the harassed authorities were compelled to call in the army, who promptly dynamited the cave entrance and sealed it off.

Possibly the most colourful and fondly remembered character ever to live in Lakeland was one Millican Dalton. Born near Alston in 1867, the early part of his adulthood was spent in London, where he worked in a shipping office. But he craved a freer life and he became a guide, working in the Lake District, Scotland, Epping Forest and Switzerland. There can be no better testament to the beauty of Borrowdale than the fact that of all the splendid places he knew, he returned here every summer.

Following the example of a hermit from the distant past, he made his home in a cave on Castle Crag. A vague inscription he made in the rock can still be seen there. A Quaker and strict vegetarian, he was content to fend for himself, even baking his own bread. He also made his own clothes, which were of eccentric appearance, usually consisting of shorts, tweed coats and tyrolean hats decorated with herons' plumes. Very proud of his frugal existence, he maintained that everybody else spoiled themselves with pampered living. The only luxury he allowed himself was an old eiderdown which he found to be of great comfort.

He gave lessons in raft building, sailing and rock climbing, all skills in which he was self-taught. Known as 'Professor of Adventure', his popularity grew to such an extent that he was soon a tourist attraction in his own right. A photograph of him aboard his wonderfully ramshackle raft *Rogue Herries* became a best-selling postcard.

Millican's greatest ambition was to sail his raft through Borrowdale on the river into Derwent Water, on through Bassenthwaite Lake and then to the Solway Firth. He died at the age of 80 in 1947 without ever completing the voyage.

Borrowdale provides the base for two walks to surrounding tarns which superbly demonstrate the outstanding beauty of the area.

STYHEAD AND SPRINKLING TARNS

The tiny hamlet of Seathwaite is as far south as one can travel into Borrowdale by road. Statistics say that it is the wettest inhabited place in England, with an average of 131in (3,327mm) of rain per year. An even higher count is measured at the head of the valley at Styhead and Sprinkling Tarns. The prevailing westerly winds carry moist air over the highest mountains in England just beyond the tarns, and the air cools to form clouds and rain. But please don't let this deter you. High rainfall does not mean persistent rainfall, and I have spent many glorious days here swimming and camping at the tarns.

Because of the exceptional beauty of the area and the close proximity of the highest mountains, many visitors are attracted to Seathwaite. For some it is a base for the ascent of Scafell Pike, England's premier peak. Others come here with the same intention but travel no further than Sprinkling Tarn, captivated by its charm. And that is exactly how I was introduced to the place. The long lane that leads to Seathwaite provides parking for many vehicles, but if you are planning a visit during a summer weekend or bank holiday, you will nevertheless have to arrive early to find a spot.

The route begins at some farm buildings and passes over a footbridge by the small campsite. Following a beck upstream, our initial ascent is gentle, over boulder-strewn ground. The wide, rocky bed of the stream is evidence of the torrents that come down from the mountains after cloudbursts. The path is faced and flanked by high, rugged peaks as the valley falls away behind.

Some patches of wet ground are forded by stepping across the boulders, and then we arrive in view of Taylorgill Force. The waters of Styhead Gill fall through this 140ft (43m) cascade in a wooded ravine between the precipitous lower slopes of Base Brown and

Styhead Tarn, Great End and an inquisitive local on a warm
summer morning. Viewed from Green Gable

63

Seathwaite Fell. The sight of the falls is as sudden as the sound, and if an early morning start has left you a little groggy, you will surely now be wide awake.

The path leads up on the right of the falls, hugging the steep wall at the base of some crags, and then climbs out of the ravine. The gradient eases considerably now as the ascent continues alongside Styhead Gill. This is a classic Lakeland mountain stream, tumbling over smooth rocks interspersed with small, glistening pools. If the day is hot, it is a joy to splash around and quench one's thirst in the cool, rushing water. To the rear the view of Borrowdale grows longer, seen through the V-shape formed by Base Brown and Seathwaite Fell.

The giant of Great End looms ahead with Great Gable on the right and then Styhead Tarn appears at their feet. The tarn sits among the mountains at an altitude of 1,430ft (436m), just below the highest point of Styhead Pass, an ancient thoroughfare linking Borrowdale with Wasdale. The name of the pass derives from Old English words that refer to the hill over which it travels. Previously, it was known as Hederlanghals, an amalgamation of Old Norse and English, referring to the rapidly flowing stream issuing from the tarn.

In quite recent times the authorities put forward the idea of building a road through here. To visit the place is to know just what a ludicrous proposition that was, and needless to say the idea was laughed out of court.

The deepest part of the tarn has a solid rock base covered by about 30ft (9m) of clear water. From north-east to south-west it measures about 250yd (225m) and it is 150yd (140m) wide. Over the centuries, deposits from the gully between Great and Green Gables have partially dammed the tarn, raising the original water level. It is fed by streams from Great Gable, Styhead Pass and Sprinkling Tarn and contains a few brown trout. There are four tiny beaches dotted around the shore, which is easily accessible for the most part, but becomes a little marshy around the inlet streams at the southern end. The ground around the outflow is best for camping.

Although one would expect Great Gable to figure prominently, the overriding impression is of the dominance of Great End standing guard over the tarn. It is to the lower slopes of this mountain that the path now leads. As we head up the well-trodden track to Sprinkling Tarn, another path branches away to the right. This is part of the well-documented Corridor Route which enjoyed great popularity in Victorian times. In those days, tourists didn't venture far without knowledgeable guides and they were often led this way, skirting around Great End and Broad Crag on the way to, and back from, Scafell Pike. On my very first solo walk in the Lake District, I too found myself on this path, under a blazing sun in perfect visibility. No excuses then for the fact that I was nowhere near my intended route, hopelessly lost!

It is only on the ascent towards Sprinkling Tarn that Great Gable begins to assume the majestic appearance one expects of it, and Styhead Tarn is left behind as our path climbs alongside one of its feeder streams. At the top of the rise, Sprinkling Tarn appears so suddenly that one almost walks straight into it. It is one of the most enjoyable tarns in Lakeland, possibly the very best. Discuss the tarns with any experienced walker and more than likely Sprinkling Tarn is the first one that comes to their mind.

Like Styhead Tarn, Sprinkling Tarn is a relatively modern name. It was previously known as Sparkling Tarn, a title that should have endured, as it perfectly describes the jewel-like body of water. Before this it had yet another name, Prentibountern, which is commonly believed to relate to a local outlaw who was hanged nearby. In fact the word is derived from Old English and means 'Sparkling Stream'.

The tarn rests on a rocky ledge formed by Seathwaite Fell, at an altitude of 1,960ft (597m). The waters are held in check by moraine which ancient glaciers brought down from the Scafell range. The large boulders and rocks of the moraine have settled over the years and become embedded into soil and vegetation. Now the tarn is surrounded by thick grasses and numerous rocky outcrops which constantly rise and fall over the length of the ledge, offering countless small hollows for exploration.

Wandering northwards along the ledges, just beyond the tarn one comes to the broad ridge of Seathwaite Fell. Here, hidden amongst the rocks, is another small tarn, and carrying on towards the end of the ridge above Aaron Crags, there are at least a dozen more tiny little pools with a view back to Borrowdale and the distant fells.

Although the shore of Sprinkling Tarn itself has many comfortable camping locations, this area among the knolls and rock pools provides a greater sense of adventure and freedom. Certainly, you won't be bothered by anyone else.

In keeping with the complex character of the ridge, Sprinkling Tarn has a particularly interesting shoreline, boasting numerous bays with small promontories, and is approachable most of the way around. On the north-western section, a long peninsula reaches out into the water leaving just a narrow channel between itself and the eastern side. North of this, the shore opens out again to form a shallow harbour containing a small rock island. Anglers will probably find this area the most productive. The small brown trout here are swift, cunning and plentiful.

From east to west the tarn measures about 260yd (240m) and about 160yd (150m) from north to south excluding the harbour-like bay. All this adds up to an ideal location for swimming and drying off on the sun-kissed rocks. I remember a late September day when I saw a small group of young men enjoying the water. Apparently, they had been given the choice of a Mediterranean holiday or a visit to the Lakes. Some of their associates had chosen the former, but these few had opted to come here. They couldn't believe their good fortune to be swimming and sunbathing so late in the year when they had expected merely a walking holiday. They were busy with their cameras, eagerly anticipating showing off holiday snaps to incredulous friends back home. I heartily agree with their sentiments; give me Sprinkling Tarn on a good day and you can keep the foreign beaches.

As one would expect, the water is beautifully clear, and it has a maximum depth of 30ft (9m). It is fed by an inlet stream from Great End that runs through a small patch of marsh near the shore. Once again, the towering walls of Great End dominate the scene, the harsh, broken gullies and loose rocks providing a contrast to the softness and light of the tarn. There is an almost reverential silence about the place, in keeping with its position in the lap of the upper echelons of the Lakeland mountain kingdom.

The path away from Sprinkling Tarn heads up towards the peaks, but we do not go that far, turning instead across Ruddy Gill.

Above: Sprinkling Tarn viewed from the lower slopes of Great End

The soil of the gully that brings the stream down to us has a high content of iron, giving it a strong red hue. The source of the stream, Esk Hause, is just 500ft (150m) above. This is the pivotal col of the Lake District. Connecting the Scafell range with the long Glaramara Ridge and Esk Pike, it is the focal point of all the major valleys and their mountain ridges.

Having easily forded the beck, our path climbs a few feet to the top of the gully and presents a stunning view. At our feet, Ruddy Gill has cut a deep ravine into the rock, through which can be seen Borrowdale, Derwent Water and Keswick. Beyond all these, the Skiddaw group of mountains cap the picture.

The path follows the course of the gill now, leading back to Seathwaite. Although there is a long descent, the going is comfortable on a well-maintained path, and interest is kept high by the various falls and pools in the beck. Ruddy Gill is crossed by footbridge, after which it flows into Grains Gill. Some of the pools on the way down are very inviting and the best of them comes at Stockley Bridge. Large enough to hold a small group of bathers, and usually about 10ft (3m) deep, this is an incredibly attractive rock pool. Children (of all ages) simply cannot resist it. Possibly the finest of its kind in Lakeland, its crystal water passes through smooth bleached rock and has just a hint of blue.

Soon after this, the beck merges with Styhead Gill and then we come back to the farm buildings and cottages at Seathwaite. Meals, ices and sweets are available here in the tea rooms and café.

This walk can be completed in a little over two and a half hours if you make no stops but there is so much to enjoy that I recommend that you set aside a full day at least for the journey. Some of the climbing is steep, but never excessively so. The path beside Taylorgill Force is precarious in places, but the rest of the route is straightforward.

A late summer morning above Ruddy Gill, looking towards Borrowdale, Derwent Water, Skiddaw and Blencathra

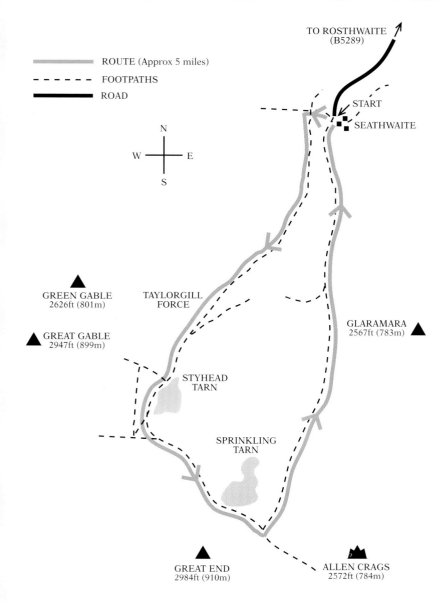

ROUTE (Approx 5 miles)
- - - - FOOTPATHS
ROAD

TO ROSTHWAITE
(B5289)

START

SEATHWAITE

N
W E
S

GREEN GABLE
2626ft (801m)

TAYLORGILL
FORCE

GREAT GABLE
2947ft (899m)

GLARAMARA
2567ft (783m)

STYHEAD
TARN

SPRINKLING
TARN

GREAT END
2984ft (910m)

ALLEN CRAGS
2572ft (784m)

ROUTE SUMMARY

MAP:	OS Outdoor Leisure Maps 5 and 6
START:	Seathwaite, Borrowdale, GR 235122
DISTANCE:	Approximately 5 miles (8km)
TIME:	2½ – 3 hours
DIFFICULTY:	Care must be taken in the Taylorgill Force ravine

ROUTE DIRECTIONS

To reach the start of the walk, take the B5289 through Borrowdale, and head down the valley towards the Honister Pass. Just before Seatoller hamlet, a lane turns to the left heading to Seathwaite.

1 Among Seathwaite's farm buildings, you will see an archway on your right sign-posted 'Footpath and Campsite'. Go through the archway and then cross the footbridge.

2 Turn left immediately after the footbridge through the gate, following a path alongside the beck, which leads up to Taylorgill Force.

3 Moving along the path in the ravine, watch out for a fork to the right. It is easy to take this fork inadvertently, but it leads steeply up to the crags and then peters out. You should keep to the path that leads to a fence and tree line that drops alongside the waterfall in front of you.

4 After the ravine, the path carries on alongside Styhead Gill. Another path joins from the left over a footbridge and you then come to Styhead Tarn. The path runs alongside the shore.

5 Bear left around the top (southern) end of the tarn and move up the slope with Great End on your right and the stream on your left.

6 The path arrives at Sprinkling Tarn, following the southern shore. After the tarn turn left, off the main track, into the gully and across the stream, following Ruddy Gill down.

7 Go straight on when a path branches off to the right.

8 Cross the first footbridge and eventually you will come to Stockley Bridge.

9 Go through the gate here and cross the bridge, after which the path leads down to Seathwaite.

WATENDLATH AND DOCK TARNS

The largest of the settlements in the heart of Borrowdale is Rosthwaite. From here we begin the second walk in the area. Approximately 4½ miles (7km) in length, this route is designed to suit all the family; the total walking time amounts to only about two and a half hours.

Our route leaves Rosthwaite via a road leading to the Hazel Bank Hotel, a building featured in the 'Herries' novels by Sir Hugh Walpole. He bought a house near here on his first visit to the Lake District, and grew very fond of walking in the immediate area. He was particularly enamoured of Watendlath Tarn, describing its many moods in detail.

The path follows an old pack horse route that was once the main thoroughfare linking Borrowdale with the east. As we climb steeply over the wide, stony track, a view of the valley opens out behind. The south-western reaches of the dale stretch out to Seathwaite and include all the fells around the Honister Pass. The first ascent is soon over, flattening out on Puddingstone Bank. We are only 1 mile (2km) into the journey and yet the outlook has changed character completely. Now our surroundings are of open moorland with only the breeze for company. Soon the path starts to descend and presents Watendlath hamlet ahead, with its tarn on the right.

The entire Lake District is well conserved, with modern 'improvements' being accepted reluctantly – and very often flatly rejected. But if there is one spot in the National Park that time could be said to have passed by totally, then Watendlath is it. A route centre in the days of pack horses, the hamlet's name is believed to mean 'the Barn at the End of the Lake'. Today it still consists only of barns, the tarn and a handful of cottages. One of these caters for visitors as a tea room, with a delightful tree fringed garden. But accommodation here is very limited, and at the end of the day the visitors are gone, leaving the locals to themselves.

This is a favourite location for landscape artists, and they are often seen clustered around the ancient stone bridge over the outflow beck, which blends perfectly with the stone built homesteads. Most visitors arrive by way of a narrow road that comes up the valley from the north. On the way this passes over Ashness Bridge, which must be the most photographed place in rural England. On postcards, calendars, books and map covers, wherever images of Lakeland are sold throughout the world, you will find a picture of this bridge with its view of Derwent Water and Skiddaw.

Then the road threads through a valley of rock outcrops, hollows and woods overlooked by heather topped ridges, before terminating at the National Trust car park in Watendlath. To many visitors it must seem as if they have reached the end of the world. They can travel no further (except on foot) and they can see no further, as the tarn and hamlet are surrounded by fells. These encroach closest on the eastern and western sides; on the latter side a deep wooded gully climbs steeply towards High Tove. A couple of farm ponies are usually in evidence near Watendlath's bridge, along with goats, geese and ducks. Many of the fowl are wild but they mingle contentedly with their domesticated cousins, and all of them will be more than happy to share your lunch.

A fence crosses the outflow beck at the edge of the tarn, and provides the only harsh aspect to the whole view. It is a necessary intrusion however, as it prevents the tarn's rainbow and brown trout from escaping. Stocked annually by the National Trust, they grow to very good weights. Rainbows seem to be the most common. They certainly form the bulk of catches, but perhaps they simply lack the cunning of brownies. Only fly fishing is allowed, and permits are available from Fold Head Farm, Watendlath.

Left: Summertime, and the walking is easy. Looking down on Rosthwaite in Borrowdale from the path to Watendlath

there small pockets of heather hint at the bonanza that lies in store. A short steep climb leads up close to the head of a small canyon and Skiddaw appears in the distance, way beyond Watendlath.

Soon the path arrives at the top of the rise and leads onto the undulating shelf of Great Crag. Suddenly we are in a different world. All around is a sea of vibrant purple/red heather interspersed with grey and white rock outcrops. Here and there the greens of grasses and brackens show through. On a fine day, blue and white from the sky enhances the picture. As the path winds through this wonderland Dock Tarn appears ahead, reflecting the light of the sky at an altitude of 1,320ft (402m). A mass of multi-hued water lilies add to the spectrum, and the russet and gold of reeds and a few small trees complete the riot of colour. The name Dock Tarn means the 'Tarn of the Water Lilies'. Of course the scene I have described can only be witnessed from late summer to early autumn, when the heather is in full bloom.

This is the only tarn where such a splendid sight still exists. Until 1994 there was another one at Lingmoor above Langdale, but now that area has been burnt off in an attempt to increase grazing. Many parts of the Lake District have been treated similarly in the past, but instead of fresh grazing only fern covered slopes have resulted – very colourful in the autumn and winter, but no substitute for glorious heather. Please stick closely to the path, and don't damage one single scrap of the precious stuff. It is the National Trust we can thank for the preservation of Dock Tarn's surroundings and long may they rule.

Realistically, Dock Tarn cannot be enjoyed in any way other than as a spectacle. The water is for the most part very shallow, with only two or three places deep enough for bathing. It is inadvisable to attempt to reach these spots, as it would result in the disturbance of mud and silt on the bed, rendering the exercise pointless. However,

The tarn itself measures about 340yd (310m) from north to south and 220yd (200m) from east to west. The ground around the southern shore is marshy where Blea Tarn Gill feeds in, and it is usually at the shallows of this section that most anglers congregate.

The memory of Watendlath will stay with you long after your visit. It is not just the tranquillity of its perfect rustic setting, there is something more, an intangible quality that can best be described as haunting.

As the path rises away to the south en route to Dock Tarn, Watendlath is reluctant to leave our view, seeming to call us back. We pass over an area of wetlands that have been protected by a stone path, making the passage comfortable and unmistakable. Here and

Above: A quiet morning at Watendlath, looking south at the pack-horse bridge and the tarn

Looking south from one of the many heather-topped crags around Watendlath's valley on a late summer afternoon

reeds, tantalising evidence, perhaps, of what lies unseen.

The maximum depth of the tarn is about 15ft (4.5m). It measures around 270yd (250m) from north to south, and half that distance across. There is one tiny island near the north-western shore, and a number of small promontories break the overall oval shape. From higher outcrops around the tarn hollow, a view to the south shows the great valley of Langstrath pointing to a backdrop of mountains around Bowfell. To the west the undulating heather-clad foreground is topped by yet more distant peaks. The outflow runs down Willygrass Gill, followed by our path, still surrounded by small crags and heather. A deep gorge opens on the left and then the path arrives above the densely wooded slopes overlooking Stonethwaite hamlet, nestled in the south-easternmost reaches of Borrowdale. This is the best viewpoint of the day, looking over the valley between Ullscarf and Eagle Crag, then Langstrath followed by the steep north-eastern slopes of the Borrowdale Fells. To the right of this, Dale Head, High Spy and Maiden Moor lie behind the main body of Borrowdale. On paper, it is not the most impressive collection of fells, but from this viewpoint, they form a spectacular panorama.

There follows an extremely steep descent through the woods on a stone path. On a summer or autumn evening the heading is straight into the sun and the passage through the woods is illuminated with dappled light and intermittent dazzling flashes as the sun peeps momentarily through the canopy.

Down in the valley our path joins a section of the Cumbria Way. Seventy miles (112km) long, this path links Ulverston with Carlisle, passing along the way through some of Lakeland's most popular valleys.

Down in the fields and dry stone walls once more, we arrive at the beautifully clear Stonethwaite Beck, which at this point is almost as wide as a river. Shortly after joining the beck we arrive back at Rosthwaite.

there are a few locations where you can cool off your feet and perhaps even step out a few yards without kicking up a murky cloud. This restriction will not detract from your enjoyment – after all, some places are there to be seen not touched.

I am told that the water holds some trout of a respectable size but I have only ever noticed very small shadows darting around the

Above: Late autumn at Dock Tarn, looking from the western shore towards distant Skiddaw

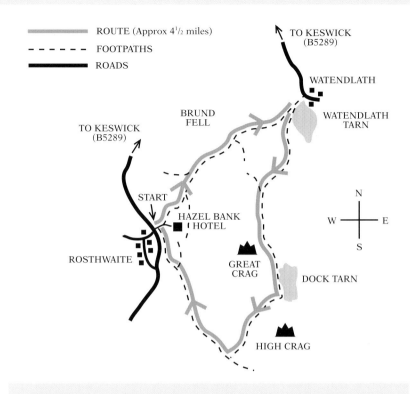

ROUTE (Approx 4½ miles)

FOOTPATHS

ROADS

TO KESWICK (B5289)

WATENDLATH

BRUND FELL

WATENDLATH TARN

TO KESWICK (B5289)

START

HAZEL BANK HOTEL

ROSTHWAITE

GREAT CRAG

DOCK TARN

HIGH CRAG

N
W · E
S

ROUTE SUMMARY

MAP: OS Outdoor Leisure Map 4

START: Rosthwaite, Borrowdale, GR 257148

DISTANCE: Approximately 4½ miles (7km)

TIME: 2¼ – 2¾ hours

DIFFICULTY: None

SPECIAL NEEDS: Fishing permit for Watendlath Tarn,
                 available from Mrs Richardson, Fold Head
                 Farm, Watendlath

ROUTE DIRECTIONS

In Rosthwaite there is a car park down the lane opposite the village post office.

1 Walk back towards the post office and turn left on the main road.

2 A few yards up the road, you will see the access road to the Hazel Bank Hotel on your right. This is signposted 'Public Bridleway, Stonethwaite, Watendlath'. Follow the track up to the bridge over Stonethwaite Beck where two tracks cross.

3 At this point, follow the sign 'Public Bridleway Watendlath', skirting to the left of the hotel grounds.

4 Pass to the right of a farm gate and go through another gate.

5 After a second gate, a faint path branches right. Our way is to the left on the more obvious track, and up the hillside.

6 At the top of the ascent, on Puddingstone Bank, another cross-track is reached. Go straight on here, again following the major track, which leads to Watendlath.

7 The path goes alongside the tarn's western shore following a sign 'Public Footpath Dock Tarn'.

8 Moving away from Watendlath, a series of direction indicators point the way. The fourth marker also says 'Dock Tarn' and points to the left.

9 A series of posts mark the route now, which leads over some marshy ground and then up to Dock Tarn. At the tarn, the path passes alongside the western

shore and then follows the outflow beck, eventually leading down through woods into the valley.

10 At the bottom of the descent, turn right where the path forms a T with another path that runs alongside a wall.

11 When you reach a bridge on your left, go straight on following the sign 'Public Bridleway Watendlath via Rosthwaite'.

12 Next comes a fork in the track where the right branch goes to Watendlath. Bear left here, crossing the bridge, and follow the path back into Rosthwaite.

CHAPTER 9

HARROP TARN & BLEA TARN

THIRLMERE

A summer afternoon at Harrop Tarn, looking towards Tarn Crags from the route alongside the northern shore

On the A591 between Keswick and Grasmere, travellers pass through a 4 mile (6.5km) section between the steep, forested slopes of Helvellyn and Thirlmere Reservoir. Across the water, more steep, wooded slopes rise up to Armboth Fell, completing a classic Lakeland scene.

The absence of any settlement on or near Thirlmere's shore ensures that it attracts only a fraction of the visitors one would expect at such a large and well situated water. The fact that it is a reservoir might act as a deterrent to many people, or perhaps it is the lack of obvious access points on the shore alongside the A591.

A minor road runs through the woods on the western shore, and it is along there that the finest access spots can be found. Picnic areas abound, fishing is free, and at the Armboth car park there is a launching area for rowing or sailing boats. Powered boats and swimming are prohibited by North West Water in order to protect the water quality.

Although the area has always been known collectively as Thirlmere, it was formerly the site of two lakes: Wythburn Water and Leathes Water. In 1879 Manchester Corporation purchased both lakes and their catchment area: a total of 11,700 acres (4,735 ha). The flat bottomed lake valley, with its beautifully clean waters, presented an ideal opportunity for reservoir construction. In 1878, the Bishop of Manchester said, 'If Thirlmere had been made by the Almighty expressly to supply the densely populated district of Manchester with pure water, it could not have been more exquisitely designed for the purpose'. Construction began in 1890 and was completed four years later. Only a very small dam was required to bring the water level up sufficiently for extraction, a rise of 54ft (16.5m). The two lakes became one, and their overall length was extended by about 1½ miles (2.5km).

The water travels 102 miles (163km) to Audenshawe's reservoirs in south-east Manchester, through an ingenious array of underground conduits, pressure pipes and overland aqueducts. At no point along the journey are pumps used; gravity and air pressure are the only driving forces. In more recent times, the system was extended to supplement Cumbria's and central Lancashire's supplies.

When Manchester Corporation took charge here in 1879, the surrounding area had been deforested. The trees had all been taken to Keswick to produce charcoal for smelting copper and lead. Extensive coniferous planting began in 1908, and now there are about 2,000 acres (800ha) of woodland, much of it commercially operated. Since 1982, North West Water and the National Park Authority have worked to develop public access and wildlife conservation whilst enhancing the landscape.

The fruits of their labours can be enjoyed over the first section of our circuit, and again on the final leg of the journey. This is one of the longer routes, covering a distance of about 7½ miles (12km). There is no major difficulty with climbs or descents if adequate time is taken. Between three and a half, and four hours walking time is needed, so a minimum of five hours should be allowed, including rest periods.

THE WALK

The walk begins at Dob Gill car park on Thirlmere's western shore, stepping immediately into the forest. A stone path winds up steeply through mixed woodland, thickly carpeted in pine needles and cones. After levelling out, the path passes close by Dob Gill Waterfalls, and then, while still within the woods, arrives at Harrop Tarn.

The tarn's hollow forms a shelf on the long sweep of land down from Ullscarf to Thirlmere. Its altitude is 950ft (290m) and is held by glacial moraine covered in grass and marshes. Beyond the flat, boggy edge, woods surround the clearing on three sides, with the eastern side sparsely occupied by fresh saplings. Unfortunately, these have been damaged by very determined sheep, which resist all efforts to keep them out.

Harrop Tarn is gradually silting up. Deposits come in through three streams, and it is vital that North West Water's efforts to create a balance between new and mature trees is successful. This would slow down and eventually stop the erosion. Reeds around the shore are encroaching at an ever-increasing rate, and the water is becoming shallower. In the four years that I have known the tarn there has been a noticeable reduction in its surface area. At the time of writing, the shoreline measures approximately 220yd (200m) from east to west and 110yd (100m) from north to south. The recorded maximum depth is 15ft (4.5m), but I suspect that has diminished over the years.

It would be nothing short of tragic to lose this beautiful water; few tarns have such a richly forested setting. Even on the southern side, where the land rises up precipitously to crags, there is a broad covering of trees between the base of the crags and the tarn's clearing. On summer days, the clearing is filled with warmth and light, and the tarn glitters in its emerald setting, shielded from the world by its surrounding woods. Although it is difficult to reach the shore in most parts, the north-western corner offers some firm ground around the narrow inlet stream. Here, one can while away many pleasant hours in the sleepy hollow. Trout and perch cause an occasional splash or ripple in the water, while the quiet humming of bees and dragonflies form a constant lullaby. A glance up to the crags will often reveal a buzzard or two circling high or swooping down to skim the treetops. At twilight, red deer come down to the shore from the woods and the surrounding fells. They can often be seen on the southern shore, across the water from the main path.

After leaving Harrop Tarn, the route continues to rise through woodland, until it reaches a double gate that marks the boundary

between forest and open fells. Going up between Standing and Bell Crags, a wide view begins to unfold to the rear, where open fell leads down to the forest. Beyond the unseen Thirlmere, Helvellyn's rounded western slopes and skyline lead on to Nethermost Pike, Dollywaggon Pike, Seat Sandal and Fairfield.

As we climb higher, and begin to move across a high plateau, the rear panorama gradually recedes and then disappears. Immediately, another opens out ahead, incorporating the Derwent Fells, the Skiddaw range and the sea. After a few more paces, Blea Tarn is revealed beneath us, with its north-western tip pointing directly at distant Bassenthwaite Lake.

There are no steep, overhanging crags to darken Blea Tarn. It sits in a basin at 1,560ft (475m) on the open moorland, held in place by moraine. The ground rises gradually from the western side up to Coldbarrow Fell, but on the whole there is nothing to prevent the sky from illuminating this very large tarn. It measures about 560yd (510m) in length from north-west to south-east and 260yd (240m) at the widest point. The shoreline is easily accessible all the way round, apart from one or two spots on the western side where the last few feet of ground drop steeply into the water. The western and southern shores are the most interesting, with a number of small beaches and headlands. On the long eastern shore, the grassy surroundings are flat, and a little marshy in places.

An inlet stream comes down from Ullsgarth, passing between Coldbarrow Fell and Standing Crag before entering the tarn on the southern shore. An outflow goes from the pointed north-western tip, en route to Watendlath Tarn. Camping and fishing is best along the north-western side, where an occasional rocky knoll and generally steeper ground provide dry, firm locations. There are a good number of trout here, some of a very respectable stature. A few small perch share the water, which reaches a maximum depth of over 40ft (12m).

The northern vista from Coldbarrow Fell: Watendlath Tarn, Derwent Water, and Bassenthwaite Lake

The tarn's spacious setting provides rich rewards for those who want to spend some time exploring the surroundings. From Coldbarrow Fell there is a breathtaking view over Watendlath Tarn, Derwent Water and Bassenthwaite Lake to the sea. But I would advise you not to stray too far up the hillside above the eastern shore. Close to the fence that runs along the skyline, there are some patches of bog waiting to trap the unwary, as I found out when my legs disappeared up to my thighs.

The path leads away from Blea Tarn, up to the high ground of Watendlath Fell. Initially the ascent is wet underfoot, then reaches some cairns where the going is far more comfortable. Those who have studied their Ordnance Survey maps might be tempted to find a way down from here to Thirlmere, by way of Launchy Gill. However, no matter what you might think the map suggests, there is no footpath that way, and certainly no right of way. Furthermore, to attempt such a route would disturb the red deer herds which graze

Above: The close of a hazy summer day at Blea Tarn.
Viewed from Standing Crag

from the world. A solitary tractor busies itself in small fields around the tarn, pursued by enthusiastic sheep dogs. Their sounds and the occasional bleating of sheep are all that break the silence. A pair of rowing boats drift slowly, fishing lines betraying the course of a breeze that causes silver ghosts to flit momentarily across the water.

One cannot stay here for ever, however; there is still a good distance to travel. After crossing the highest point of the moor on High Tove, the path skirts to the left of a deep recess. Beyond this, the ground rises in a series of high rocky knolls, bedecked with purple heather. Look for red deer along the horizon formed by the tallest pinnacles, assuming that they have not seen you first.

There is total silence as the path descends through a steep gully. Helvellyn reappears ahead, and then sounds begin to drift up from Thirlmere and the road. We re-enter the tree line as the gully becomes very steep. Here, a fence provides a welcome handrail over the most precipitous section, and then we are back once more at road level. Cutting across the road, the route enters a car park and picnic area, then passes on to the shore of Thirlmere at the launching site. From here, North West Water have opened a permissive path that follows along the shoreline to Dob Gill. This is broken only in one 30yd (25m) section, where it is necessary to walk along the road.

Before that section, water laps gently on the rocky shoreline, as our path passes within the woods. We pass two islands along the way, with Helvellyn's western slopes dominating the skyline. It can be a little awkward underfoot in places, as the path continually rises and falls, although this final leg is never strenuous. However, if you feel that you have had enough for one day simply turn right through the woods, and you will come to the minor road that is deceptively close at hand. Eventually, the path enters a clearing at Dob Gill and turns up to a gate. Through the gate and across the road lies the car park.

in the valley. It is better therefore to carry on in a northerly direction from the cairns. This leads towards the rugged skyline of the Derwent Fells, where the whole western horizon is filled by a seemingly endless array of jagged peaks. Bassenthwaite Lake grows ever clearer to the north-west, pointing at the sea, as the path continues on high, open moorland. All around are multicoloured grasses, bracken, heather and rocks. Soon, Watendlath Tarn appears below, with Grange Fell in the background ablaze with heather.

Up here, where the path turns sharply to the east, is a marvellous spot to take a breather. A refreshing beck cuts across the way then passes through a steep gully to the tarn, over 400ft (120m) beneath us. Watendlath presents a timeless picture, ostensibly cut off

Above: Looking northwards along Thirlmere from the lakeside path, on a still autumn morning

ROUTE DIRECTIONS

Turn off the A591 on the minor road for Armboth, and park at Dob Gill.

1 From the rear southern corner, a path leads up through the woods. At the beginning of the path, you will see signs describing both a green and a white route.

2 The path remains both clear and uninterrupted until you reach Harrop Tarn, where a wide track cuts across the way. Turn right, following the sign marked 'White Route'.

3 After the tarn, the track bends sharply to the right where a lesser path branches to the left. Take the left branch, which then joins another wide track.

4 Here you will see a sign 'Public Bridleway Watendlath'. Follow the Watendlath marker and ignore the 'White Route' sign.

5 About 100yd (90m) further on, there are direction markers on each side of the track. Someone has scratched 'Blea Tarn' on the right-hand marker; follow the lesser path that branches to the right, and up the wooded slope.

6 Soon you will arrive at the point where another track branches to the right. Follow the 'Bridleway' sign here, keeping straight on.

7 The path reaches a double gate at the boundary of the forest and the open fell. Go through the gate and carry on upwards along the most obvious path. Ignore any lesser paths that you might see branching to the right.

8 At the top of the rise, the path crosses a narrow plateau and then a gate appears ahead. Through this the path is unclear, but Blea Tarn can be seen below. Head for a point about 30yd (25m) to the right of the eastern shore until you find the path.

9 Follow it along the shoreline to the outflow beck.

10 Here you will see a sign 'Footpath to Watendlath', which points up the hillside towards a large cairn on the horizon (heading north-north-west). A series of small cairns mark the way up to it, across marshy ground.

11 From the large cairn, another series of cairns mark the path to Watendlath. They are very widely spaced, but for the most part the path is clearly visible. Eventually it arrives at a gully stream immediately above Watendlath Tarn.

12 Here, on your side of the gully, a sign says 'Armboth'. Turn sharp right, following the direction of the sign, heading to the east.

13 Now the path begins the final ascent of the day, up to High Tove. Slightly beyond the highest point, it passes through a gate and then begins to descend towards a gully, through which Helvellyn can be seen. The way becomes unclear in places, but carry on towards the gully where once again the path is obvious.

14 A very steep descent leads down to the road. Turn right here and then almost immediately left to the car park signposted 'North West Water Armboth Car Park'.

15 Go through a gate and down onto the open shoreline.

16 Turn right now (south), to pick up a path through the trees.

17 At Launchy Gill a path branches sharply to the right. Go past it and continue along the shore.

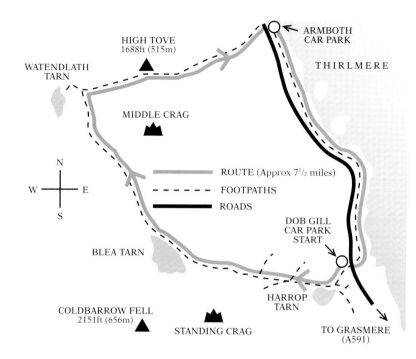

18 Further along, the path leads up to the road, which it follows to a gate on the left signposted 'Lake Shore Path Dob Gill'.

19 Go through the gate and continue along the path until it enters a clearing and bears up to the right alongside a stream. This leads to the road opposite Dob Gill car park.

ROUTE SUMMARY

MAP:	OS Outdoor Leisure Map 4
START:	Dob Gill car park, GR 316140
DISTANCE:	Approximately 7½ miles (12km)
TIME:	3½ – 4 hours
DIFFICULTY:	Some steep climbing (one hour), and one very steep descent

On maps of the Lake District all the lakes appear to radiate out from a central hub, similar to the spokes of a wheel. Close to the centre of the hub – right in the heart of Lakeland – lies Grasmere lake and village.

The wool and mining industries were chiefly responsible for the growth of Grasmere, but now it is the centre of the tourist trade. Many people believe that it is the most picturesque village in England. Others find it a little too perfect, lacking that 'lived in' look. However, it is certainly the most popular place among Lakeland's visitors; a constant throng mill around its oddly arranged streets and lanes. In every direction there are street cafés, tea rooms and restaurants mingled with antique shops, craft shops, bookshops and outdoor clothing centres. There are hotels, inns and guest houses to suit every taste, and almost everything is built in red and green Lakeland slate. Trees dotted around the buildings and gardens complete the picture postcard image.

The village and lake nestle in a green valley surrounded by peaks. The best known of these is Helm Crag, famous for the rock configuration on its summit. When viewed from certain angles in the valley, the summit rocks assume the shape of 'the lion and the lamb'. This can be seen to good effect from the main road between Town End and the Swan Hotel.

St Oswald is believed to have preached here in the seventh century, after which the village church was built and dedicated to him. In the churchyard are the graves of William Wordsworth and his family, and it is Grasmere's connection with the Lakes' poets that attracts so many visitors today.

In the two walks from Grasmere we will visit Wordsworth's main residence and explore the fells and tarns of an area that inspired him and others to write their immortal lines.

CHAPTER 10

GRASMERE

High summer at Easedale Tarn, viewed from our route near Great Castle How. The Helvellyn range forms the horizon

Left: Grasmere village and the fells around Easedale on an autumn morning, viewed on the route to Alcock Tarn

ALCOCK TARN

Of the various locations in the Lake District that have connections with Wordsworth, Dove Cottage at Town End is by far the most important. This is the first objective on a short walk that involves a steep ascent of around thirty minutes' duration, after which one can take it easy for the remainder of the journey.

There are numerous car parks in Grasmere village, but because of the constant stream of visitors I cannot recommend any particular one. The route therefore begins at the Red Lion Hotel opposite the post office, in the centre of the village.

The road passes St Oswald's Church and Grasmere Sports Ground, with a first glimpse of the lake over to the right. After crossing the main road we step onto the lane in Town End, a fairytale hamlet constructed entirely of Lakeland stone and slate. Dove Cottage and its attendant museum, shop and restaurant are all here, just a few yards up the lane.

William Wordsworth and his sister Dorothy had always hoped to share a home of their own. After renting a number of houses in the south of England, they came to Dove Cottage shortly before Christmas 1799, returning to the Lake District, where they had spent the early part of their childhood. Coleridge and other poets were regular visitors, and Coleridge moved to the Lake District from the south in order to continue working with Wordsworth on 'The Recluse'. Together with Dorothy Wordsworth, they would walk the fells and row on the lakes whilst composing their poetry.

William settled down to what he considered to be his vocation of making the world a better place by instilling a sense of appreciation of the environment through his poetry. The next eight years proved to be the most productive of his life. It was largely due to work accomplished here that he was catapulted to national eminence and feted by his fellow poets. Despite setbacks such as the death of their brother and a worsening relationship with Coleridge, both William and Dorothy were blissfully happy. In 1802 William married, but life carried on as usual, even when the children started to arrive. Most of the documentary evidence of the Dove Cottage years is provided by Dorothy's chronicles of the period.

In the summer of 1808, the Wordsworths returned to Dove Cottage after a lengthy visit to London. William was still in mourning for his brother and the mood of the household was further dampened by the loss of some family friends and neighbours killed in a mountain fall. The cottage was getting too small to house the growing family and reluctantly it was agreed that it was time for a change. Later that year they moved across the valley to Allen Bank. More changes of address followed in later years but the happiness and creativity that William enjoyed at Dove Cottage were never to be rediscovered.

The lane carries on after the cottage and museum to How Top, after which we pass along a gravel path and through an area of enormous rhododendron bushes. Much of the land here is cared for by the National Trust and is beautifully maintained. A steep, winding path leads up to a small walled pond built by a previous landowner. We can thank the same person for our path. It is much better than the older one, which lies on the far side of a wall over to the right. I had intended to take the route that way, but found that for much of the ascent the high wall obstructed the views of the valley. On the improved route, the path snakes up through trees and once above the tree line, Grasmere comes into view.

As we climb higher the views open out to present a spectacular scene and shortly before reaching the tarn, Grey Crag marks the best viewpoint of our walk. To the north, the road to Keswick climbs into the distance over Dunmail Raise. As the eye moves southwards the 'lion and the lamb' are followed by Easedale and High Raise.

Right: Looking south towards Windermere as Alcock Tarn
sparkles in summer sunshine

Beneath us lie Grasmere village and the lake with a backdrop of high ridges and peaks. During autumn the changing colours of bracken and woods on facing hills contrast with the perennial green in the valley. The southern aspect, showing Windermere and its surrounding lowland, completes the picture. There is something reassuring about Grey Crag. From its position above the valley and the main thoroughfare, it seems as if it stands guard, keeping a watchful eye over the village and passers-by.

In his touching poem 'Michael', Wordsworth writes of a cottage built high on the steep slopes of the fell close to Grey Crag. Michael was a shepherd, working every day on the fells with his son. Each night his wife Isabel placed a lantern in the cottage window to guide husband and son home. The lantern could be seen by everyone in the valley and became known as the 'evening star'. It had a cheering effect on the locals, becoming a symbol of the life and love of country folk. As long as the 'evening star' shone brightly, all was well. It cannot be said with certainty which cottage or site Wordsworth was describing. Perhaps it was entirely fictional. But there is no doubt that he was writing about the area of Grey Crag and the affection that it inspires.

In August you might see red flags dotted around the peaks and the slopes here. They mark the route taken by fell runners on the day of Grasmere Sports. This is a major event in the Lakeland calendar, with a wide range of traditional contests in athletics, wrestling and hound trails. They are held on the third Thursday after the first Monday in the month.

A little further on the path passes through a gap in a wall and arrives at Alcock Tarn at an altitude of 1,170ft (357m). There are no steep surrounding slopes here. The tarn is held in place by moraine on the western shore and by the small dam at the southern end, through which a narrow outflow is allowed to escape. An inlet stream comes down from Heron Pike and enters at the south-eastern tip.

The eastern shore is flanked by a wall, beyond which lie masses of ferns interlaced with faint tracks. I have often seen people wandering around the bracken trying to find a clear track to the summit of Heron Pike. Unfortunately, there is none from the immediate vicinity of the tarn.

Roughly finger shaped, the tarn measures about 200yd (180m) from north to south by 50yd (45m) at its widest point. The width fluctuates in the crooks of the finger. The maximum depth is only 8ft (2.5m) and would be considerably less but for the efforts of a Mr Alcock, who dammed the water in the late nineteenth century. Prior to this the tarn had been named after Butter Crag which lies slightly to the north. After building his dam, Mr Alcock stocked the tarn with rainbow and brown trout. Now only the brownies remain and they are plentiful, if a touch small.

The position of the tarn on a shelf about half way up the slopes of Heron Pike gives it an open air and the sky is reflected brightly on the shimmering surface. To look at it on a map suggests that it might offer a good view of Grasmere. But the bulk of the containing moraine prevents that. The best outlook is to the south facing Windermere.

The shore is most easily accessible near the dam, where you can find a series of tiny beaches. On the open ground around the southern reaches there are many flat, grassy places that make this a popular picnic spot for family groups. It is indeed a very pleasant place to spend an afternoon after visiting Dove Cottage.

On leaving, the path descends steeply, heading for a gully stream. There comes a charming, shaded section of the route as it passes beneath trees alongside a dancing beck and then on down a leafy lane between some very desirable cottages. The beck cascades beside us, filling the arbour with sound, and then we are out on a minor road that leads down to the Swan Hotel. From there we re-enter the village, passing by a blacksmith's, and then on into the centre.

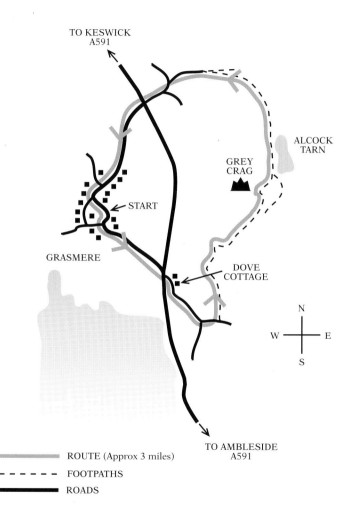

TO KESWICK
A591

ALCOCK
TARN

GREY
CRAG

START

GRASMERE

DOVE
COTTAGE

N

W   E

S

TO AMBLESIDE
A591

—— ROUTE (Approx 3 miles)

- - - - - FOOTPATHS

—— ROADS

ROUTE DIRECTIONS

1 From the Red Lion Hotel in the village centre, head towards St Oswald's Church and the Garden Centre.

2 Cross the bridge and pass a large car park on your left.

3 On reaching the main road cross over and go up the facing lane to Dove Cottage.

4 After the cottage, carry on up the lane until you arrive at a fork. Go to the left, where a sign says 'No through road for motors'.

5 You will then see another sign 'Public Footpath Alcock Tarn' pointing up a gravel path to your left. Take this path, going past a bench.

6 This leads to a fork in the path, take the left branch through a gate.

7 As the path starts to rise, you will see a branch down to the left. Go past this, staying on the main path and climbing.

8 This leads up to Grey Crag. Carry on from there through a gap in the wall and on to Alcock Tarn.

9 The path runs along the tarn's western shore to a stile.

10 Over the stile a steep descent leads to a footbridge and then on to a lane. At the bottom of the lane, turn left on the road and then right at the fork.

11 The lane leads down to the main road. Across the road you will see Swan Lane. Go down the lane and back into the village centre.

ROUTE SUMMARY

MAP:	OS Outdoor Leisure Map 7
START:	Grasmere village, GR 337075
DISTANCE:	Approximately 3 miles (5km)
TIME:	1½ – 2 hours
DIFFICULTY:	None

ALCOCK TARN

CODALE AND EASEDALE TARNS

The second walk from Grasmere covers a distance of approximately 7½ miles (12km), taking in both Codale and Easedale Tarns. Although there is no great difficulty involved, about four and a half hours is needed to cover the route, which may be too much for inexperienced walkers. However, family groups can leave the main route between Great Castle How and Blea Rigg, descending to Easedale Tarn and then back to Grasmere. This shorter walk eliminates a two-hour section that includes Codale Tarn, but is nevertheless an enjoyable outing.

On both routes the bulk of the climbing comes in the first ascent to Silver How, with the remainder a little later, going up to Great Castle How. On other sections altitude is gained almost imperceptibly. For those taking the longer route, a little scrambling might be necessary on the steep descent between Codale and Easedale Tarns.

Beginning from the small car park in Easedale Road, our route goes a little way down the road and then crosses a field. Soon we join a metalled lane through a pleasantly wooded section. To the right is a view of Grasmere's northern surroundings, including Helm Crag, Heron Pike and the ridge leading to Fairfield.

The leafy lane leads to two cottages, after which we are on a footpath of stone and shale where the main ascent begins. Our path quickly passes on to the open hillside and after crossing a gully stream, the summit of Silver How comes into view.

At an altitude of 1,292ft (394m) Silver How commands a wide and varied view. The eye is caught mostly by Grasmere lake and Rydal Water, with Windermere, Elter Water and Loughrigg Tarn completing the aquatic picture. Around all these are a multitude of peaks and ridges. To the west and north lie Bow Fell, the Langdale Pikes and Helm Crag. Looking gradually eastwards, we see Helvellyn and its companions, then the Fairfield Ridge with Grasmere village at its feet. Coming back towards the west, the panorama is completed by Wetherlam and the mountains around Pike of Blisco.

Grasmere has such an extensive reputation and Silver How is so obviously a fine viewpoint of the immediate area, that it attracts a truly cosmopolitan gathering. There were Canadians, Americans, Australians, Dutch and French there on my latest visit. Around lunch time I spoke to a gentleman from Colorado, after which we went our separate ways. Seven hours later I was re-entering Grasmere when I bumped into him again. He was heading back to Silver How with some friends in tow, determined that they should not miss the view. Even for a man from the Rocky Mountains, this area holds such an attraction. It was the colour of the landscape that most fascinated him, so rugged and yet so green.

From Silver How the route crosses the broad ridge that separates Great Langdale from Easedale. It winds through undulating ground composed of innumerable rocky knolls, grassy saddles, shelves and minor crags. The breadth of the ridge provides a foreground for distant mountains and curving valleys, which appear first to one side and then the other. This is a time-consuming section of the walk but also very enjoyable. It is one of those classic Lakeland ridges that give the walker a strong sense of adventure, completely separated from the world below. Most of Grasmere's visitors are left behind now and one's thoughts are free to wander.

Along the way our path arrives at the site of an unnamed tarn above Great Langdale. Although it is marked clearly on maps, it is overgrown with reeds for most of the year and during the summer it almost dries up completely. I believe that it is drying out progressively from year to year and that it will disappear eventually. From here Langdale is seen sweeping away into Oxendale, with the Langdale Pikes and Bow Fell capping the view.

Left: A perfect autumn afternoon on Silver How, overlooking Grasmere and Rydal Water

As the path continues along the ridge, glimpses of the Helvellyn range appear intermittently to the north. Soon we reach the point where we can choose between the long and the short routes. Easedale Tarn lies far below, with a background of four mountain ridges culminating in Helvellyn. From here a path leads down to the tarn's southern shore.

For those taking the full route, a path continues up the rocky face of Blea Rigg. Harrison Stickle and Pavey Ark appear ahead and to the left as we approach Codale Tarn. Slightly before the descent to Codale begins, a detour of just a few paces towards the edge of the ridge unveils a wide open and extensive view. Both Codale and Easedale Tarns can be seen clearly, with the land rising from Codale's western shore up to High Raise. Ullscarf in the Wythburn Fells lies due north, while Helvellyn and the long Fairfield Ridge sweep down beyond Easedale.

Now the path makes a steep traverse of Blea Rigg's north-western slope down to Belles Knott. Minutes later we arrive on the southern shore of Codale Tarn. The glacier that reached down from High Raise to Easedale deposited large quantities of moraine. To the north and west of the rocky outcrop known as Belles Knott a natural dam was formed that now holds Codale Tarn. It is set apart from the main mountain routes and only those walkers who make a point of visiting the water know of its charm.

Located at 1,520ft (463m) in the upper reaches of a valley that descends in steps to Easedale and Grasmere, the tarn usually comes as a pleasant surprise to people who see it for the first time from Blea Rigg. Measuring about 220yd (200m) from north to south and exactly half that from east to west, the clear water reaches a maximum depth of about 25ft (7.5m) and contains many perch with a few trout. The ground can be marshy around the southern shore, where the tarn is shallow, but firmer ground and deeper water are found on the other three sides. A solitary feeder stream comes in from the north, and the outflow is at the south-eastern corner. From the waterside the outlook is of enclosing mountains on three sides, with quite high moraine on the fourth side leading to Slapestone Edge. But steep slopes encroach closely only on the western side, so the surface is relatively open to the sky, and is a deep shade of blue. In summer the water temperature can be surprisingly high, cooling at a slower rate than its surrounding ground. I have known days at Codale when the weather has turned cold and overcast, making bathing unlikely. However, on testing the tarn I have found it to be much warmer in the water than out in the mountain air. The eastern shore provides some comfortable camping spots, and although you might have occasional visitors during the day, it is doubtful whether you will be disturbed at night.

Our next objective is Easedale Tarn, over 600ft (180m) below en route to Grasmere. The path accompanies a beck flowing down from High Raise, passing through the greater part of the descent very quickly. After heavy rain this can be a tricky section and it might be necessary to use your hands in order to avoid slipping, but after about ten minutes the gradient eases. Codale Tarn's outflow splits into two streams above us, which then merge with the main beck on our left. A look back up the way we came shows them cascading down the fellside in an impressive picture dominated by the high pointed profile of Belles Knott. It is a surprising scene, as there has been no hint previously of how compelling Belles Knott can appear. Nor does one realise how far the route has descended from Codale Tarn until one stands here at the foot of the waterfalls.

At this point there is a shallow combe to the right of the path that looks as if it should contain a tarn. Indeed it used to do so, but the water long ago dried up. Some effective work has gone into maintaining the path that lies between here and Easedale Tarn. Now the

Right: An October morning on the route across Blea Rigg, overlooking Codale and Easedale Tarns

way is comfortable and very pleasant as it approaches a large combe containing the tarn.

Because of its proximity to Grasmere, Easedale serves as an introduction to the Lakeland tarns for many people, myself included. It is a delightful playground for young and old. Long, lazy days can be spent on its shores, the best locations being along the northern side, beneath the towering backdrop of Tarn Crags. Here the ground is firm and dry, with an interesting shoreline of bays and beaches. The water becomes deep quickly on this side. In some places it is possible to dive straight in, but always beware of submerged rocks. The safest bathing is at the beaches. The eastern shore is also worthy of exploration, crossing the containing moraine to the southern side, where the ground is open and largely marshy.

An old sheepfold near the northern beaches offers the best camping site, but really one is spoilt for choice. The tarn has long been a favourite with walkers, and at least two enterprising people have in the past taken advantage of this popularity. A local innkeeper served teas from an old hut, keeping the approach path in good repair to encourage customers. He even carried a boat up to the tarn and hired it out. Later, another man sold soft drinks from the same hut. Unfortunately it no longer exists.

This is one of the largest tarns. It measures about 530yd (480m) from east to west and 330yd (300m) from north to south. The water has a maximum depth approaching 70ft (20m), and contains many perch and eels with some brown trout. A large part of their food is provided by masses of minnows, which are always in evidence in the shallow water on the southern side, and very close in on other shores, chased there by hungry mouths. Enormous damsel flies are a common sight here, their incandescent blue torsos hovering perilously close to the surface of the water.

The surrounding ground falls steeply to the water on the north-eastern, northern and western sides. Much of this high ground is formed by Tarn Crags and Slapestone Edge. On the southern side the outlook is far more open, leading up to Blea Rigg and Great Castle How. The remainder of the surround is formed by deep moraine, through which the outflow beck Sourmilk Gill wanders down into Easedale. The main feeder stream is the one we followed to the tarn. A number of others come in from the south over marshy ground and two more flow down from Tarn Crags. A solitary rock island lies about half way between the northern and southern shores and a third of the way from the eastern side. I am told that the best trout can be found around there, if one could only reach them.

Sourmilk Gill follows our path down towards Grasmere, resplendent with waterfalls and rock pools on steep sections of the descent. Down in the valley the flow of water assumes a relaxed pace, passing through a long shaded section beneath trees. It presents a classic English brook scene, and if one ventured no further from Grasmere than this, it would still make an enjoyable outing.

After passing through a final piece of woodland, the path emerges onto Easedale Road opposite Oak Lodge. Teas, ices and soft drinks are available here, and can be enjoyed in the garden while you admire the design and the red Lakeland slate of the lodge.

There is a permissive footpath, avoiding the road, a little way down from Oak Lodge. A two-minute walk along it brings us back to the car park.

ROUTE DIRECTIONS

Easedale Road goes north-west off the B5287 through Grasmere. A short distance up the road you will see a small car park on your right.

1 Walk back from the car park down the road towards Grasmere.

2 After about 200yd (180m) there is an iron farm gate on your right signposted 'Public Footpath Score Crag, Langdale'. Go through the gate and alongside the wall and fences on your right.

3 Another sign saying 'Footpath Langdale' points to the right where you join a metalled path.

4 This leads up to two cottages where you will find a sign for 'Silver How, Langdale'. Go through the gate on your left following the sign. The metalled path gives way to stone and shale now.

5 After passing through another small gate you will see a minor path branching to the left following the course of a stone wall. At this point move away from the wall on the major path that leads steeply upwards.

6 Pass by two cairns and then bear left where the path forks.

7 Soon you will find a gully immediately to your left. Walk alongside it until you see a faint track branching down to the gully stream. Follow this and cross the stream on the stepping stones.

8 Shortly before reaching the summit of Silver How, the major path branches left into a cleft. The right branch is not as obvious but the summit can be seen clearly, so go to your right up to the summit cairn.

9 To continue from Silver How head towards the west – in the opposite direction to Grasmere Lake. The first section of our path is unclear, so ensure that the lake is behind you.

10 The path becomes a little easier to see and then reaches a fork near a small pool. Take the left fork, but do not approach the pool. Bear to your right, away from the pool and continue along the more obvious path, which leads to a tiny tarn.

11 Walk past it on the right hand side and you will come to a much clearer path that cuts across your way. Turn left here.

12 Soon you will see the unnamed tarn (or at least the site of it) near Lang How on your left. Continue past it, and when the path forks take the left branch.

13 After a few minutes you will come to a shallow stream where once again the path forks. Take the major branch to your right and upwards. Now the path leads up and over Little Castle How, then down and up once more onto Great Castle How.

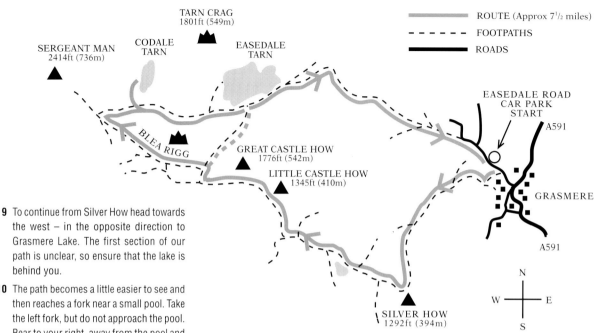

Continued over page

ROUTE SUMMARY

MAP:	OS Outdoor Leisure Maps 6 and 7
START:	Easedale Road car park, Grasmere, GR 334080
DISTANCE:	Full route approximately 7$\frac{1}{2}$ miles (12km)
	Short route approximately 5 miles (8km)
TIME:	Full route 4$\frac{1}{2}$ – 5 hours
	Short route 2$\frac{1}{2}$ – 3 hours
DIFFICULTY:	Very steep descent between the tarns on the full route

14 Soon you will pass two tiny tarns on your left. Then the path enters a wet, peaty section. Skirt around this and head for a small mound topped with a cairn that lies ahead of you.

15 After this you will approach a steep rise. When you see the rise ahead, bear to your right across the open area, and look straight ahead (north).

16 About 100yd (90m) away you will see two boulders topped with tiny cairns. The boulders are spaced about 6yd (5.5m) apart, and they mark the path that leads down to Easedale Tarn.

17 Those taking the longer route to Codale Tarn should turn left, up the steep face of the rise where the other path goes down to Easedale Tarn.

18 Continue along the ridge-top path. Wherever the path forks, bear right. Remember that your route closely follows the edge of the ridge on your right and that you must not stray to the left.

19 Eventually you will reach the cairns at a cross-path on the col between Blea Rigg and High Raise. From here turn sharp right (almost doubling back on yourself) and down towards the tarns.

20 Although it is not marked on Ordnance Survey maps, there is a clear branch to the left 500yd (450m) into the descent. This leads to Codale Tarn.

21 From the tarn, return to the main path and turn left to go straight down towards Easedale Tarn.

A winter's day at Oak Lodge on Easedale Road

22 Near the tarn the path forks. The left (fainter) branch leads to the northern shore and the right (major) leads to the southern. This is the point at which those who took the short cut rejoin the main route.

23 To leave the tarn go to the southern side of the outflow stream, and follow it down on a very clear path. After a steep descent this leads into the valley.

24 Immediately after crossing a narrow footbridge you will see two gates ahead. Go through the one on the left signposted 'Grasmere'.

25 After another gate the path crosses another footbridge in a copse of trees, and then comes out onto Easedale Road. Turn right along the road until you see a sign on the right 'Permissive Path Avoiding Road'.

26 Take this path through a field beside the road until you reach a stile on your left. The stile is directly opposite the car park at the end of the route.

Great Langdale lies in the very heart of the Lake District. Beginning near Elterwater, it cuts a broad swathe through the mountains for about 4 miles (6.5km), heading to the west where it terminates in the two long fingers of Mickleden and Oxendale. Pike of Stickle, Harrison Stickle and Pavey Ark are known collectively as the Langdale Pikes, and are distinctive landmarks which dominate the valley and can be seen for miles around.

Three routes venture into the mountains and combes from Great Langdale, the second and third of which begin at the western end. Before reaching that far, the valley road passes through the village of Chapel Stile. Here, there is a well stocked store for those who have forgotten any items of equipment or need to replenish supplies. From the village, the road enters the main valley and arrives at a group of buildings that include a hotel, the New Dungeon Ghyll Inn and the Sticklebarn Tavern. The first route begins from here. It is a very popular location with climbers and walkers, especially younger ones who make use of the bunk house facilities at Sticklebarn Tavern. During the summer, it can be a very lively place, particularly when local blues bands are performing.

STICKLE TARN

There are a number of car parks around the Sticklebarn Tavern, and any can be chosen as a base for our walk to Stickle Tarn. Although the route covers a distance of just 4^1/$_2$ miles (7.2km), it is a very steep and high-level one. The journey should only be attempted by experienced walkers, and will take between three and a half and four hours. On leaving the car park, Stickle Ghyll's waterfalls catch the eye, as they crash down from the tarn's combe beneath Harrison Stickle's towering heights. The steep climbing begins immediately after we leave the tavern and hotel. Our first objective is Dungeon Ghyll Force,

CHAPTER 11

GREAT LANGDALE

On Pike of Stickle at daybreak, looking towards Harrison Stickle and mist-shrouded Great Langdale

a 100ft (30m) waterfall that cuts through a narrow ravine. The path climbs alongside the ravine as a wide panorama begins to unfold. The Langdale Pikes are temporarily obscured by the steep slopes on which we stand, but looking from the west to the east we see Crinkle Crags, Oxendale, Pike of Blisco, Little Langdale with Blea Tarn, the full length of Great Langdale, and finally Windermere.

After the initial steep climb, the gradient becomes gentler and the pikes come back into view. Then another climb brings us to a slight hollow between the pikes and Loft Crag. Between Loft Crag and the unmistakable pinnacle of Pike of Stickle, very steep screes fall down to Mickleden. Quite recently, it was discovered that the screes mark the site of a Neolithic 'factory' where axe heads and other cutting implements were shaped before being sent to Ravenglass. From there, they were transported around the British coastline or exported to Ireland and Brittany. All this occurred as much as 5,000 years ago, and many historians have expressed surprise at the organisation and enterprise of the operation. A sign at the mouth of the screes requests that people should not descend that way, to avoid damaging the site. One glance at the gradient is enough to deter sensible walkers.

All the Lakeland peaks have cairns on their summits, but the one on Pike of Stickle appears as an extension of the pinnacle itself as we approach it. There is a timeless aura about this peak, most keenly felt early in the morning when mist fills Mickleden far below, and the mountains to north, west and south protrude above a white 'sea'. Even though Pike of Stickle's summit stands at 2,326ft (709m), Great Langdale is obscured beyond Harrison Stickle and Loft Crag until the route crosses over to Harrison Stickle, where the full eastern panorama unfolds once more. Stickle Tarn lies almost 900ft (270m) below the rock strewn summit, which stands at 2,414ft (736m). This is the highest point of the route, which heads to the north from here, over Pavey Ark. The path passes to the left of Stickle Tarn's deep combe, which remains out of sight behind various knolls and crags until a steep descent over loose stones brings us to the tarn's north-eastern inlet stream, and then to the shore.

Stickle Tarn is one of the most popular in Lakeland. Casual walkers are drawn here by the attractive path that leads straight to it alongside Stickle Ghyll's waterfalls. The falls themselves are a magnet for those hardy types who can often be seen climbing mountains, not by the way of any path, but up through the streams. Other walkers pass this way en route to the pikes, many of them climbing up through Jack's Rake, Lakeland's most famous scramble, which leads up and across the almost vertical face of Pavey Ark that forms the tarn's enormous western wall. On other sections of Pavey Ark, climbers are often seen where no paths or footholds could possibly exist, ascending by means of ropes and pitons.

Pavey Ark completely dominates the combe, its sheer face descending into piles of rock and scree before reaching the shore. To the south-west, it gives way to Harrison Stickle and then the land swoops down to form a thin strip around a dam. Above this, the Coniston Fells, Wetherlam and the Furness Fells can be seen in the distance beyond Great Langdale's southern fells. This open, southern aspect, makes Stickle Tarn's combe very warm whenever the sun shines, and a favourite place for swimming. Although the surroundings are not so steep on the eastern side, they still rise to a considerable height. To the north they climb up to Sergeant Man, and offer effective shelter from any wind.

The National Trust owns Stickle Tarn's surroundings, but the water itself is the property of the National Park Authority, which is responsible for the upkeep of the dam at the southern tip. This was constructed to provide an emergency water supply for the old Elterwater village gunpowder factory, and was used whenever Great Langdale Beck was too low to power the factory's machinery.

The tarn itself measures approximately 460yd (420m) from north-east to south-west and 300yd (270m) across. It lies at an altitude of 1,540ft (469m) and its beautifully clear water reaches a maximum depth of around 50ft (15m). The dam is built on vast deposits of moraine which originally held the tarn in place. A couple of minor feeder streams come in from the east, but the main inlet pours down from Sergeant Man, entering at the north-eastern corner, near a tiny rock island. The shore is easily accessible all around, apart from a small section where the minor inlets come in. Elsewhere it is firm and dry, with many large boulders scattered around the water's edge beneath Pavey Ark.

Shoals of minnows can be seen in the shallow water close to the dam and the eastern shore. They provide the staple diet for Stickle Tarn's numerous brown trout. These fish move around the tarn in

Above: An autumn morning on Harrison Stickle. Blea Tarn and
Pike of Blisco lead on to the fells around Coniston

shoals, and it pays the angler to move around the shore until one hits a hot spot. This can result in a very rewarding fifteen minutes or so until the bites stop and then it is necessary to relocate the shoal.

There are some good camping sites to be found here, particularly above the eastern shore near a tiny peat moss tarn, and above the path on the southern side.

From the tarn all that remains of the route is a steep descent on the footpaths alongside Stickle Ghyll. At one point, the path passes very close to a spot where you can step across to the head of the tallest waterfall, and sit above the precipice looking out over Great Langdale. Eventually, the path returns to the inns and hotel. Sticklebarn Tavern has a large patio with a good view of the valley. Meals and drinks can be taken here, at the end of a somewhat tiring, but extremely rewarding day.

Above: A glorious summer morning above Stickle Tarn. Harrison Stickle and Pavey Ark are reflected in the water

ROUTE DIRECTIONS

The B5343 branches off the A593 at Skelwith Bridge near Ambleside. It leads through Chapel Stile into Great Langdale, and about 2 miles (3km) into the valley arrives at a small group of inns, cottages and a hotel on the right-hand side of the road. There are three parking areas available, a free one to the left of the road, one owned by the National Trust on the right, and the inns' own parking spaces.

1 From whichever car park you choose, find Stickle Cottage at the rear of the inns.

2 To the right of the cottage there is a gate and a sign marked 'Public Bridleway'. Having passed through the gate, bear left up to a gap in a wall and then on to an opening in a fence.

3 After the fence, a path joins from the left and then forks. Take the left branch up to a gate.

4 Turn right immediately after the gate, following the wall on your right.

5 The path leads up to a stile and then forks again. Take the left branch down to Dungeon Ghyll, and follow upstream with the beck on your right.

6 As the path climbs steeply, keep watching for a track which branches sharply to the right through the ferns. This leads to the ravine and Dungeon Ghyll Force. From there, rejoin the main path.

7 The ascent continues up to two cairns where the path forks once more. Take the left branch that leads up to a string of three cairns.

8 Here, the path splits at the top of the rise, in a slight hollow between Pike of Stickle, Loft Crag and Harrison Stickle. Bear left up to Loft Crag, and then onto Pike of Stickle.

9 From there, head due east, down into the hollow, and then up to Harrison Stickle.

10 Care should be taken over the next section to ensure that you do not stray to the right, close to the edge of the combe. Many paths have been formed over the years along the broad ridge of Pavey Ark. It is very easy to take the wrong one and attempt to descend to Stickle Tarn by way of Jack's Rake. Although many people enjoy the climb up this narrow ledge, it is almost impossible for all but skilled climbers to go down it. Therefore, from Harrison Stickle locate the path that runs north-north-west.

11 Continue along this, ignoring the first path which branches to the right.

12 At the next fork bear right, and then right again at a third fork. If at any point on this section you find yourself beginning to pass over the lip of the combe, turn back and relocate the main path, for it is certain that you have taken a false track. Eventually, the path drops down a steep gully on loose stone and shale.

13 After crossing Bright Beck, follow the path to the right, down to Stickle Tarn.

14 At the tarn's north-eastern corner another path branches to the left. Bear to the right here, and continue along the shoreline to the dam.

15 Descend to the left of the outflow and keep close to the stream. Another path branches away from it and descends to Sticklebarn by a slightly higher route, but

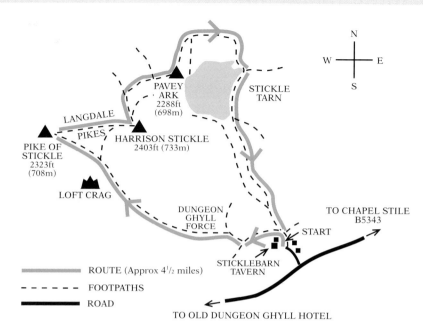

this is a far less interesting path, so be sure not to stray from the stream at the beginning of the descent.

16 Some way down a tiny section of the path is lost under water and it is necessary to cross and then recross the stream.

Alternatively, you could continue the descent on the opposite side, or even start from the opposite side at the dam.

17 Eventually, all the paths converge and return to the rear of the inns and cottages.

ROUTE SUMMARY

MAP:	OS Outdoor Leisure Map 6.
START:	Sticklebarn Tavern, Great Langdale, GR 294064
DISTANCE:	Approximately 4½ miles (7km)
TIME:	3½ – 4 hours
DIFFICULTY:	High level route. Steep climbs and descents

STICKLE TARN

THREE TARNS AND ANGLE TARN
(BOW FELL)

The Old Dungeon Ghyll Hotel lies beneath the Langdale Pikes at the head of Great Langdale. The public bar has an old-world charm and down-to-earth simplicity that climbers and walkers find irresistible. They come here after their day on the fells to eat and drink around the log fire, comfortable in the knowledge that muddy boots or clothing will leave no stain on the smooth floors and wooden benches. It is a place of warmth and laughter, tall tales and folk songs   a rare survivor of a bygone age.

There is a large campsite operated by the National Trust close by, ideally situated for those who wish to stay in the valley after walking the two routes that begin and end at the hotel's car park. At least four hours is required for the walk to Angle Tarn, which covers a distance of around 7½ miles (12km). This includes two steep climbs with two very steep descents, one of which is somewhat tricky. However, experienced walkers will have no difficulty with it.

Initially, the path passes through lush, green fields completely surrounded by mountains. In this respect, Great Langdale is reminiscent of Wasdale Head. The path heads straight for Oxendale, with Mickleden branching away to the right, flanked by the towering ramparts of Pike of Stickle. After passing through Stool End Farm, the long ascent to Bow Fell begins on a wide and stony track. This climbs away from Great Langdale's fertile basin, over a long ridge formed by The Band. Crinkle Crags, Great Knott and Pike of Blisco rise up beyond Oxendale to our left, while the screes of Pike of Stickle's Neolithic axe factory appear almost vertical to our rear.

As more height is gained, a detour of a few paces to the right reveals the enormous S-shape of Mickleden where it joins Great Langdale, which then sweeps away to the south-east. Soon, the gradient eases and Great Langdale disappears behind The Band. The path can be seen for a long distance ahead, leading up to the col between Crinkle Crags and Bow Fell. Another steep climb brings us to the col, where five major paths converge. There is our path from The Band, another from Oxendale, one coming down from Crinkle Crags, one from the mountains and valleys to the west, and yet another heading north to Bow Fell.

It is here, among hard volcanic rocks and boulders, that the tiny waters collectively known as Three Tarns offer welcome watering holes and a chance to rest before the final climb to Bow Fell's summit. Although Bow Fell and Crinkle Crags form high surroundings

Above: An October afternoon at Three Tarns, looking back towards Great Langdale. The route up to Bow Fell is visible on the left

Right: A spectacular display of mist and light, capped by the Scafells. Viewed from Bow Fell on an autumn afternoon

immediately to the north and south, both the western and eastern sides of the col fall steeply to the valleys. In both directions, only a narrow band of rocks lies between the tarns' shining surfaces and the sky. The Scafells dominate the western outlook while to the east – back where we have come from – the Langdale Pikes lead to a distant horizon formed by the northern and eastern fells.

The largest of the Three Tarns lies a few yards to the west of our path, but even that is no more than a rock pool. It does not have sufficient depth for swimming, but nevertheless holds a strong attraction for passers-by. Very few people pass the col without staying awhile, and there are many patches of grass amongst the boulders where one can stretch out and relax.

From the col, a short climb leads to the highest point of the route on Bow Fell at 2,959ft (902m). A breathtaking 360 degree panorama unfolds on the summit, where the awesomely rugged outlook is enhanced by the shattered rocks and boulder strewn ground on which we stand. In all directions, towering peaks are interlaced by sweeping valleys. Lake Windermere can be seen to the east, with the sea and estuaries to the west. Merely to list the mountains seen from here could not adequately describe the majesty of the picture. At least thirty of Lakeland's most popular fells are clearly visible, ranging from Skiddaw and Blencathra in the north to the Coniston Fells in the south. The eastern vista stretches beyond Helvellyn and Fairfield, with Muncaster Fell leading to the coast in the far west. The Scafells and Crinkle Crags are the pick of the closer landmarks, with the latter looking particularly impressive late in the day, as the sun's low rays pick out every nuance of its knolls and outcrops.

From here the route picks its way over rocks and boulders until it approaches Ore Gap, where a path leads down towards Angle Tarn. The tarn appears way below and to the right, and then our path joins the 'motorway' route from the Scafells to Langdale. After a steep descent, we arrive at the tarn's outflow beck.

At an altitude of 1,760ft (536m), Angle Tarn has all the properties one would expect of a combe tarn. Its rock basin was gouged out by glaciers, which deposited great piles of moraine between the surrounding peaks. Together, they form an almost complete bowl to hold the tarn, with just one declivity that allows the outflow beck to begin its journey into the great valley of Langstrath. A towering back wall is essential if such a tarn is to be termed 'classic' and Angle Tarn has one of the best. Bow Fell's long ridge terminates at the northern end in Hanging Knotts, the top of which stands about 1,000ft (300m) above the water. From its almost sheer upper reaches, the cliff face falls down to the rocks and scree that form the tarn's south-western shore. From there, deep moraine leads on to the slopes of Tongue Head. Continuing in a clockwise direction, the outflow is followed by Rossett Pike, then a high col that links the pike with Hanging Knotts.

The shoreline is accessible all around, even where the screes enter the water. Roughly circular in shape, the tarn has a diameter of approximately 220yd (200m) and its green-tinted waters reach a maximum depth of over 50ft (15m). It is fed by a number of minor inlet streams from the north, west and south, and by springs from deep within the back wall. Tiny beaches can be found around the perimeter, mainly near the outflow. It is a well-known stopover for walkers going to or coming back from the Scafell range, and provides a favourite camping site. The tents of groups participating in the Duke of Edinburgh's Award Scheme are often seen here, and their occupants are usually reluctant to leave. The combe's north facing aspect means that it enjoys only limited direct sunlight for part of the year, and the water can be very cold, even in summer. However, good weather and a brisk climb are all that you will need to be seduced by the sparkling surface. Anglers might find that the brown trout here are too small to keep, plentiful as they are.

Left: Angle Tarn mirrors the sky on a moody autumn afternoon.
Viewed from the route near Ore Gap

For those who wish to see Angle Tarn but are not interested in venturing onto the mountain tops, I can recommend a visit by way of Langstrath. From Stonethwaite in Borrowdale, it takes about two hours to reach the tarn. But this remarkably quiet valley has a fascination and sense of freedom that can usually be found only on the high fells. A number of deep rock pools and waterfalls line the route, and height is mostly gained very gradually. If you choose to come this way, follow the valley stream up on the western side and cross over where Angle Tarn Beck comes down from the high ground. You will find this approach much more comfortable than the one to the east.

From the tarn, it would be a simple matter to head for Mickleden by way of Rossett Gill, but I am not alone in finding that a tedious route. Our way therefore leaves the well-trodden thoroughfare and continues along the ridge top of Rossett Crag. Soon, a gully opens to the right between Rossett and Black Crags, presenting a spectacular

view down the full length of Mickleden. From our position in the gully, Langdale Fell and the pikes swoop down to the valley basin, after which The Band and Bow Fell's western slopes merge to complete a classic U-shape. The immense scale of the picture is very similar to some Scottish glens, and more than compensates for the small extra distance entailed in avoiding Rossett Gill.

A faint track traverses Black Crag before joining the well constructed footpath in Stake Gill. The descent is steep as the path zigzags into Mickleden, accompanied by the swiftly falling beck. Down in the 'glen' the path widens and flattens out completely. Bow Fell and The Band lie across the wide basin, with Pike of Stickle towering above us to the left. From here, the path skirts around the Langdale Pikes, remaining flat and comfortable throughout the length of Mickleden. On entering Great Langdale, a very slight rise in the path leads through farm gates and then down to the rear of the Old Dungeon Ghyll.

Above: A September morning in Langstrath, on the alternative route to Angle Tarn

ROUTE DIRECTIONS

1 From the Old Dungeon Ghyll Hotel at the head of Great Langdale, turn left over the bridge and then right at the lane's T-junction.

2 Where the lane turns sharp left, a postbox and farm gate lie straight ahead. A sign 'Public Footpath Oxendale/The Band' points the way through the gate. This leads through fields to Stool End Farm.

3 Pass through the farmyard and then bear left through the gate marked 'footpath'.

4 After the gate, the path forks. Take the left branch signposted 'Path to Band'.

5 Shortly afterwards, the path forks again. Take the right branch here, heading up the fellside.

6 The path remains clear and unbroken until it reaches the col of Three Tarns, where our route turns to the right and up to Bow Fell. The rocks in this area are highly magnetic, so compass readings should not be trusted. However, the path remains clear until it approaches the summit, where rocks and boulders cover the ground. The summit proper is to the left of the main path.

7 From there, return to the main path and follow the line of cairns which continue in the same direction as before.

8 Eventually this leads down to Ore Gap. In the deepest part of the gully there is a cross-path. Turn sharp right here, before the main path begins its ascent of Esk Pike.

9 Soon, Angle Tarn comes into view to the right and the path curves around and down to join the Scafell/Langdale path which leads down to the tarn.

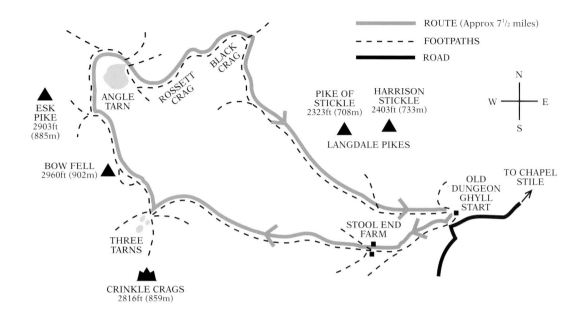

10 Go past the path that branches to the left into Langstrath, then cross the outflow beck, after which the path forks. Bear right heading up towards the col.

11 After a few paces you will come to a small section of the path that has been repaired and inlaid with large stones. Look to your left where this section ends, and you will see a faint track branching up the fellside. This quickly becomes more obvious and leads across the ridge to the gully between Rossett Crag and Black Crag.

12 Bear right into the gully, but take care to watch for the path that traverses Black Crag on your left, otherwise you will stray into the deepest part of the gully and onto steep screes.

13 Having located the path on slightly higher ground to your left, follow it across and down Black Crag. It is indistinct in places, but a series of tiny cairns mark the way until it reaches the point where the white band of Stake Gill's path can be seen clearly, winding down to Mickleden.

14 In the valley, the path widens into a flat and stony track where the path from Rossett Gill joins from the right. Continue straight down the valley, ignoring any gates that lead to the right. Follow the track all the way to the farm gate at the rear of the Old Dungeon Ghyll.

ROUTE SUMMARY

MAP:	OS Outdoor Leisure Map 6
START:	Old Dungeon Ghyll car park, Great Langdale, GR 286051
DISTANCE:	Approximately 7½ miles (12km)
TIME:	3¾ – 4¼ hours
DIFFICULTY:	Steep, tricky descent into Mickleden

THREE TARNS & ANGLE TARN BOW FELL

BLEA TARN (LANGDALE) AND RED TARN (PIKE OF BLISCO)

This, the second of the two walks from the head of Great Langdale, covers approximately 6 miles (9.5km). It takes about three and a half hours of walking time, and although there are some steep ascents, it is quite an easy route. Height is gained over four separate stages up to Pike of Blisco. From there, it is downhill all the way back to the Old Dungeon Ghyll. One section of the descent is extremely steep, so a little scrambling is necessary.

From the Old Dungeon Ghyll, the route passes through a wooded area within the boundaries of the National Trust campsite. Then it climbs steeply towards Side Pike, heading for Blea Tarn. A magnificent view of mountains and valleys opens out almost immediately. The Langdale Pikes soar above Mickleden, which is separated from Oxendale by the long ridge of The Band. This westerly view of wide valleys and high peaks has a more open aspect than is usual in the Lake District, emphasising the scale of the landscape. It has a distinctly Wagnerian feel, strongly evocative of continental mountain chains.

The path climbs up to a col between Side Pike and Rake Rigg, where Blea Tarn is revealed beneath us. A gentle descent over open ground leads into woods on the tarn's western shore.

Blea Tarn can be seen clearly from the minor road that runs beneath Lingmoor Fell, and therefore does not strictly qualify as a 'high' tarn. But to omit this beautiful place just for that reason would be pedantic, especially in view of its convenient location between Great Langdale and Red Tarn.

It lies at an altitude of 610ft (186m) in the south-western corner of a small valley or basin between Great and Little Langdales. A high knoll known as Tarnclose Crag stands at the southern shore, after which the land falls steeply towards Little Langdale. The western side is wooded around the tarn's shore, then rises precipitously to the craggy heights of Blake Rigg. To the north, the land is open, with a covering of grasses and bracken before reaching the basin's boundary, where it ascends to Side Pike. This northern aspect presents one of the most popular pictures in Lakeland, with the Langdale Pikes rising beyond the col of Side Pike and Rake Rigg. The eastern side of the basin is framed by Lingmoor Fell, with its upper reaches clad in purple heather.

In the middle of the nineteeth century, Lingmoor Fell was one of the sites favoured by the fondly remembered whisky distiller, Lanty Slee. He lived at Elterwater in Little Langdale, and began his working life as a quarryman. He quickly discovered that the manufacture of illicit whisky was much more lucrative and he built up a network of stills throughout the region, with the one on Lingmoor Fell being one of the most productive. It is rumoured that some of Lanty's best customers were to be found amongst the ranks of those who were supposed to stop his activities. Certainly, he was rarely inconvenienced by anything more severe than token fines. He became so successful that he found time to make regular runs to the coast, smuggling his liquor through Ravenglass.

On the western side, where our path is carpeted in pine needles, masses of rhododendron bushes fill the woods and come down to the water's edge. In spring they are reflected alongside the Langdale Pikes on the mirrored surface of the tarn, with a rocky headland completing an exquisite scene.

Many brown trout lie within the tarn's clean waters, and they are worth catching. Anglers need a permit from Mrs Myers at Blea Tarn farmhouse, the only building in the vicinity. The southern and western shore, particularly around the headland, offer the best access to the water. Elsewhere, the ground has patches of marsh.

Left: The Old Dungeon Ghyll and campsite beneath the Langdale Pikes. Looking towards Mickleden from Lingmoor Fell

The shoreline measures approximately 300yd (270m) from north-east to south-west and 200yd (180m) across. It is roughly in the centre that it reaches its maximum depth of over 20ft (6m). Feeder streams come in from the open ground to the north and from Lingmoor Fell, while the outflow escapes from the south-western tip. Our path follows its course on the next stage of the walk.

A gentle descent over undulating ground leads to the road that travels over the Wrynose Pass. Bleamoss Beck cuts through the bracken covered slopes along the way, then heads off towards a large outcrop known as Castle Howe which stands guard over the head of Little Langdale. Because this pinnacle is so prominent, and has a name suggestive of rulers and councils, it is often mistaken for the site of Ting Mound. In fact, this ancient earthwork, which was constructed as a meeting place for tribal leaders, in effect a local government and judicial centre, lies within the boundary walls of Fell Foot Farm, a few yards to the south-east. Nowadays, Ting Mound has a slightly less prestigious function: the farmer's wife hangs out her washing on it!

On reaching the road, it is necessary to walk for a mile on tarmac. This sounds a tedious prospect, but it is no ordinary road. It leads very steeply to the famous Wrynose Pass, offering marvellous views to the rear over Little Langdale and its tarn, then across the heart of the Lake District to the far eastern fells. You will discover very quickly that the Wrynose Pass is an attraction in its own right.

At the top of the pass, an obelisk known as the Three Shire Stone marks the point where the old boundaries of Cumberland, Westmorland and Lancashire met. From there, our route leaves the road and heads up towards Red Tarn. On the approach to the tarn, views open out to the rear beyond Wet Side Edge and Wetherlam to the distant Pennines, their dark, blue-purple horizon contrasting with the greens and yellows of our immediate surroundings. Soon, the

path arrives at Red Tarn at an altitude of 1,700ft (518m).

A long, grassy saddle, sheltered by Pike of Blisco and Cold Pike, cradles the tarn. The breach between these peaks reveals Great Knott, Crinkle Crags and Bow Fell, which appear to march in line to infinity. Artists and photographers have often portrayed this scene hoping to capture its sense of timelessness. An outflow stream falls towards this majestic picture in the north-west, through a deep, red ravine, then joins Browney Gill en route to Oxendale and Great Langdale. Back alongside our route from the south-east, marshes supply water that enters through a reed- and rush-fringed shore-line. This is not a combe tarn: glacial action has left a relatively flat

Left: A summer morning at Blea Tarn. Viewed from the southern shore looking towards the Langdale Pikes

Above: A late summer afternoon at Red Tarn, looking towards Great Knott, Crinkle Crags and Bow Fell

describes a strange incident involving some friends of hers. App-roaching Red Tarn from the Wrynose Pass, they followed a clear set of footprints in fresh snow. At the tarn's shore the footprints stopped abruptly, even though the same snowfall had covered the water's icy surface. At no point could any other prints be found. The area between here and Little Langdale has often featured in tales of spectral appearances, usually relating to local quarry or mine workers who met with untimely ends.

A short but steep climb from Red Tarn leads to a narrow gully between two separate peaks on Pike of Blisco, both of which are topped by summit cairns. The one on the left (or north-west) marks the summit proper. At an altitude of 2,312ft (705m), this is the high-est point of the route. Pike of Blisco is relatively isolated from other high ground, and offers extensive views in all directions. Near to our vantage point, Lingmoor Fell and Side Pike shelter the southern side of Great Langdale. Stickle Tarn can be seen nestled in its high combe beneath the Langdale Pikes as they lead on to High Raise. Bow Fell, Crinkle Crags and Cold Pike are close at hand, towering above Red Tarn. Further afield, the southern skyline is dominated by the Conis-ton Fells. Looking eastwards, Esthwaite Water and Lake Windermere lead on to the eastern fells, with the High Street range. Passing on to the north and west, the Helvellyn massif is followed by Skiddaw, then the Scafells. Finally, Harter Fell leads on to the coast.

The Old Dungeon Ghyll and the campsite lie about 2,000ft (610m) below, and they can be seen almost all the way down on our long and steep descent. A section of this return leg requires the use of both hands and feet. We then reach the minor road that links Great and Little Langdales. The road curves around the lower slopes of Side Pike and then we are back into the peaceful, welcoming fields and sweeping valleys. Ten minutes brings us to the campsite, and finally refreshment at the inn.

saddle and only a slight hollow in the moraine to hold the very shal-low water. Surprisingly, a few trout have managed to survive here. Many parts of the shoreline offer comfortable access to the water-side, although they are interspersed by patches of marsh. Both Pike of Blisco and Cold Pike present gentle faces, coming down through grassy slopes to a shoreline that measures approximately 170yd by 60yd (150m by 50m).

This is a seldom-visited place; most walkers pass to the north on the path between Pike of Blisco and Crinkle Crags. It has a rep-utation for solitude and mystery, and is believed to be the site of another of Lanty Slee's whisky stills. The authoress Jessica Lofthouse

Above: Looking towards Windermere from the eastern cairn on Pike of Blisco, late on a changeable summer day

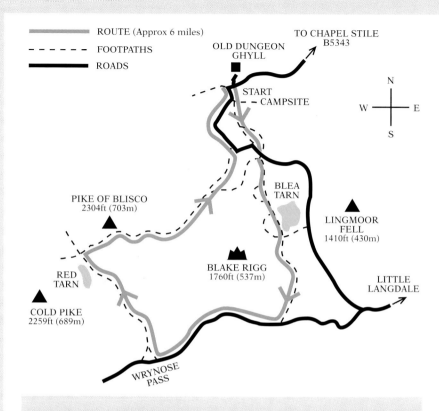

ROUTE (Approx 6 miles)

FOOTPATHS

ROADS

OLD DUNGEON GHYLL

TO CHAPEL STILE B5343

START
CAMPSITE

N
W — E
S

PIKE OF BLISCO
2304ft (703m)

BLEA TARN

LINGMOOR FELL
1410ft (430m)

RED TARN

BLAKE RIGG
1760ft (537m)

LITTLE LANGDALE

COLD PIKE
2259ft (689m)

WRYNOSE PASS

ROUTE SUMMARY

MAP: OS Outdoor Leisure Map 6

START: Old Dungeon Ghyll car park, Great Langdale, GR 286051

DISTANCE: Approximately 6 miles (9.5km)

TIME: 3½ - 4 hours

DIFFICULTY: Very steep descent from Pike of Blisco, a scramble in places

SPECIAL NEEDS: Fishing permit for Blea Tarn, available from Mrs Myers, Blea Tarn Farm

ROUTE DIRECTIONS

1 From the Old Dungeon Ghyll, turn left over the bridge, then right at the T-junction.

2 Follow the road sharply to the left at the post box.

3 Follow the 'Public Footpath' sign which points towards the campsite where the road bends towards the right.

4 The footpath runs alongside the wall on your right, branching away from the main campsite track. It leads quickly to a gate, after which the climbing begins.

5 After a second gate take a very faint path that goes straight across a small field to a stile. Still climbing through trees, it reaches another stile and then passes out onto the open fell.

6 The path follows close to the wall on your right, reaches the top of the rise, and then continues a little further to a stile on the wall. Cross the stile and then the road, to pick up the path on the other side.

7 This descends to Blea Tarn, arriving at a gate. Take the path to the right after the gate, then almost immediately turn left where the path forks. After this, the path follows the tarn's shore to the outflow beck.

8 Here, a path crosses the beck, another heads straight on to a wall and gate, and a third branches to the right. Take the centre path and go through the gate. It leads down through bracken to a point where the bracken clears and the path peters out. However, your destination is the road that can be seen clearly about 100yd (90m) ahead.

9 Turn right on the road up to the top of the Wrynose Pass.

10 A little further on from the Three Shire Stone you will see a path branching to the right (north-west), up the hillside. Follow this up to Red Tarn.

11 Just beyond the tarn a path branches sharply to the right; follow it up to Pike of Blisco.

12 On the summit, the path passes through a shallow gully between two peaks and cairns, close to the northern, or left-hand, peak. After leaving the gully, the path is faint, but can be seen curving to the right (east). Then it becomes much clearer and leads all the way down to a road.

13 Turn left on the road to return to the Old Dungeon Ghyll.

BLEA TARN LANGDALE AND RED TARN PIKE OF BLISCO

CHAPTER 12

LOW AND LEVERS WATERS

A Mountain Glory (explanation on page 113). Seen on the Old Man of Coniston, October, 1992

The Coniston region is justly renowned as one of the finest in the Lake District; it is particularly attractive to artists and writers. Tennyson chose to honeymoon here, and the area was the setting for Arthur Ransome's *Swallows and Amazons*.

On the wooded eastern shore of Coniston Water, a large house known as Brantwood occupies a site said to be the most beautiful in Lakeland, with extensive views across the lake to the Old Man of Coniston and its attendant mountains. In 1871 Brantwood was purchased by the great artist and philosopher John Ruskin, who stayed there until his death in 1900. Ruskin was the most influential figure of Victorian art, economics and social thinking. A pioneer of conservation, he foresaw the 'greenhouse effect' over 100 years ago, and was the inspiration for today's smokeless zones, green belts and town planning. The National Trust is another Ruskin brain child.

During his lifetime, Brantwood became one of Europe's leading literary and artistic centres, and Ruskin's admirers included some of the greatest names of the age, such as Tolstoy and Proust. The house is liberally decorated with his drawings and paintings, and is open to the public throughout the year. There is also a Ruskin museum in Coniston village. The most enjoyable way to visit Brantwood is by a short trip on the elegant Victorian steam yacht *Gondola* which sails from Coniston Pier, calling at the house en route to the southern end of the lake.

During Ruskin's heyday, Coniston village became Europe's most important copper-mining centre. Mining began as early as the sixteenth century, reaching peak production in the 1850s and 1860s when over 900 men were employed. Eventually, the richest deposits were exhausted, and cheap imports became too competitive. The mines finally closed in 1915. Fortunately for the local economy the closure coincided with a boom in another of Coniston's industries – slate quarrying. New workings were opened above the village, close to the

Old Man's highest reaches. The best slates could not be acquired by normal quarrying methods, and large caverns were blasted into the fellsides. Nowadays, Coniston Fells are a honeycomb of mine shafts and quarry workings, with the old machinery and buildings still very much in evidence.

The bones of the mountains have been exposed and infiltrated here more than in any other Lakeland area, leaving Coppermines Valley and the quarry workings as fascinating areas for exploration. These might not be in keeping with everyone's concept of beauty, but nevertheless their appearance and sheer scale have a stark grandeur that many people find appealing.

The return leg of our route to the tarns passes through the largest quarry to the foot of Coppermines Valley. Those who want to leave the main route and enter the valley at this point should exercise caution, and stay on clear footpaths around the shafts.

Although the route is a high-level one, and covers over 6 miles (9.5km), it could not be described as difficult. Most walkers will complete the circuit in four to four and a half hours. The ascent to the Old Man is very steep in places, particularly over the final section, but your efforts will be rewarded with stunning views. The descent to Levers Water requires some concentration. Elsewhere, the route follows clear, wide footpaths and is generally comfortable.

THE WALK

A car park stands above the grey slate buildings of Coniston village at the old railway station. From there, a tree-lined lane rises steeply alongside a gorge and stream until it flattens out where the trees clear, revealing the Old Man and the other rugged Coniston Fells. The lane continues in a gentle ascent over wide open fields, overlooked by a great semicircle of mountains formed by the Yewdale and Furness Fells, Wetherlam, Swirl How and the Old Man. Coniston Water's eastern woods come into view to the rear, with a background of distant fells.

The lane ends at a car park, which might make you wonder why it was necessary to walk this far. But to park here would entail a walk up the lane at the end of the route when tired legs would not welcome it. The alternative would be to head straight up towards Coppermines Valley from the station car park, but that would mean retracing one's steps on the return, always a wasted exercise.

From the car park, at the lane end, our route follows an old quarry track heading into the open bowl of mountains. Height is gained very gradually over wild terrain, passing through various outcrops and bracken covered knolls. Glimpses of the lake appear intermittently through the undulating ground and the vast mountain range grows ever more impressive as we enter the highest of the hillocks and knolls. Soon the track reaches the top of the rise, with a view of the main quarries directly below. The mountain bowl and Levers Water's spectacular falls frame a scene that is guaranteed to make all that pass this way stand in awe, gazing upon a picture of naked savagery.

From here, steep climbing begins on a stony track winding towards Low Water. The view of Coniston Water expands behind us and then the path enters an area of shattered stone and slate, in more old quarry workings. Steel cables line the path, with abandoned buildings and machinery on either side. A small man-made canyon and a tempting shaft lie to the left, but it is unwise to explore them deeply.

Low Water Beck's waterfalls suddenly come into view ahead, falling hundreds of feet towards the main quarry valley. Then the path leads through a series of rocky knolls to reveal Low Water at an altitude of 1,780ft (543m).

The tarn occupies a deep, dramatic combe, enclosed to the

south, west and north by the precipitous walls of Coniston Old Man and Brim Fell. Their craggy heights tower 800ft (240m) above the water. To the east, the ground falls to a ridge of rocks and boulders through which the outflow escapes. Large boulders are scattered around the shoreline, with some lying in the water, which has an unusually strong blue colour, tinted by copper-bearing rock. However, this does not detract from the pleasure of swimming here, or seem to inconvenience the native trout. A number of streams come down from the high walls, seeping through scree in places, before entering the heart-shaped tarn. It measures approximately 230yd by 150yd (210m by 140m), with shores which are easily accessible all around, and a rock basin that lies over 40ft (12m) beneath the surface at the deepest point.

From the low ridge of boulders and moraine, an extensive view includes the southern slopes of the Furness and Yewdale Fells, then on beyond the Coniston valley to Claife Heights and Lake Windermere. Looking further to the south, lowlands are capped by a distant horizon formed by the Pennines.

The high surrounding walls cut out a good deal of direct sunlight, and only in the summer months does the combe shed its rather uncompromising, hard atmosphere. At such times, it assumes a much kindlier appearance, offering countless places to laze on baking rocks and boulders, although the water remains cold. More often, however, this is a place for those who enjoy the sombre moods of mountains and their hollows. Indeed, the Old Man of Coniston has a reputation for dark, mysterious entities such as gnomes, goblins and ghosts, which are said to inhabit its innermost parts. Such legends usually originate from the days when the small, dark people of Celtic descent had to live on high ground in order to survive, forced there by a succession of invaders. The name of the Old Man of Coniston comes from a corruption of the old Celtic name *Allt Maen* which

means simply 'High Rock'. To this day, rumours hint at the existence of a religious cult which worships the mountain.

From the tarn, our path leads up to the summit. The south-eastern corner of Levers Water comes into view, capped by a series of three mountain ridges that sweep down towards the valley. As the path climbs higher, the length of Coniston Water is revealed and Brantwood is visible on the far shore. From this lofty position, the dark and light grey shapes of Coniston village appear very much like a quarry themselves, and the early section of the route through fields and high moors can be seen immediately below. Soon the steepest part of the climb brings us to the summit cairn and shelter. At an altitude of 2,635ft (803m), this is the highest point of the route.

A 360 degree panorama unfolds here, with the great bulk of Lakeland's fells to the west, north and east. But for most people, the greatest reward lies in the southern aspect. There, Coniston Water with the low fells around its southern reaches and the Torver Commons, lead on to the Duddon Estuary and the sea. On a good day, the sun gives the vast expanse of water a silvery sheen, and the Old Man of Coniston a bright, bracing atmosphere unique among these mountains.

In the spring of 1994, the Arthur Ransome Society erected a monument near the summit shelter, dedicated to the author's life and works. It overlooks Low Water's combe, very close to the spot where my photograph of the mountain glory was taken. This natural phenomenon is often confused with the Brocken spectre effect, but the two are quite different. A glory is the shadow of whoever sees it, cast onto mist in a north- or north-west-facing combe. To the south or south-east, the sky must be clear of mist and cloud. Each individual can see only his or her own shadow, regardless of how close a companion might be standing, and the shadow is encircled by a bright rainbow. The whole picture appears smaller than life-size, and be-

Left: Low Water, a fraction of Levers Water and the Coniston Fells in October. Viewed from the Old Man

neath the viewer's position. A Brocken spectre (named after the German mountain range where it was first reported) appears above the viewer's position, and can only be seen early in the morning, when the sun's rays cast shadows upwards. A gigantic shadow results, again circled by a rainbow and topped, I am told, with a halo. This is a much rarer apparition. The Old Man of Coniston and High Stile above Bleaberry Tarn are amongst the most likely places to experience a mountain glory. My photograph was taken at midday in October.

The route continues along a narrow plateau that leads down to Levers Hawse. Seathwaite Tarn and Dunnerdale come into view in the west, and Levers Water appears beneath us to the east. A steep descent follows an inlet stream to the tarn's western corner.

Levers Water is a tarn of very large proportions. Roughly square-shaped, its sides measure approximately 400yd (370m) and its depth reaches over 120ft (37m). Large boulders are dotted around the shoreline, adding to the generally rugged appearance of screes and rocks. Raven Tor, Levers Hawse, Great and Little Crags and Erin Crag provide the high surroundings on three sides, with the south-eastern section open to the sky. From here, the outflow falls down to the mines and quarries in one of Lakeland's finest waterfalls. A long dam, built to service the copper mines, regulates the flow. The dam's construction raised the water level, but Levers Water has always been a major tarn, with a solid rock basin. The clear water holds some very good trout, and the shoreline is easily approachable all the way round.

A well-trodden path comes down from Wetherlam and Swirl How, en route to Coniston, making Levers Water one of the most frequented high tarns. But this mountain combe is so expansive that no amount of people could make it feel crowded. Moreover, despite the rough texture of the surroundings, there is a particularly welcoming atmosphere here, probably owing to its position beneath crags and ridges that give shelter from the prevailing winds. On more than one occasion I have been on the Old Man in mist, cloud and howling gales, and then descended to find the tarn bathed in sunlight without a ripple on its mirrored surface.

Our route crosses the outflow and then descends on a wide track of broken stone into the quarry. Here, amongst the old levels and workings, both Levers Water's and Low Water's falls can be seen crashing down into the valley and the sense of height of the surrounding mountains is almost overpowering. There is no other corrie or high valley in Lakeland that can match this breathtaking spectacle, and to stand here and imagine what it was like before the quarries and mines carved out its guts, is enough to make anyone yearn for the paradise that was lost.

A little further down, the path arrives at a youth hostel and the Coppermines Heritage Centre. Many of the old mine buildings have been refurbished, providing self-catering accommodation for families or larger groups. Other buildings and workings have been preserved to give an impression of former life in the valley, and no matter what your feelings are about the impact of industry on the area, this is nevertheless a novel holiday spot.

From the Heritage Centre a clear path follows the course of Levers Water Beck as it falls through a series of rapids and rock pools. The deep, tree-lined gorge is crossed on Miners' Bridge and then we are back on the outskirts of Coniston village, at the Sun Hotel. The bar is open all day throughout the year and meals are served from noon till 2pm and from 6pm to 9pm. The old station car park is one minute from here.

*Left: The mirrored surface of Levers Water in September.
Looking east from the route below Levers Hawse*

*Overleaf: Below Coppermines Valley in November. Viewed from
the route near the Heritage Centre and holiday cottages*

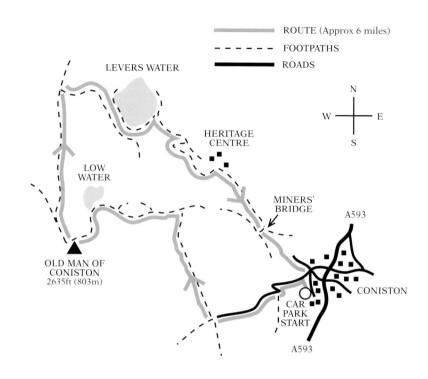

LEVERS WATER

HERITAGE
CENTRE

LOW
WATER

MINERS'
BRIDGE

A593

OLD MAN OF
CONISTON
2635ft (803m)

CONISTON

CAR
PARK
START

A593

ROUTE (Approx 6 miles)
FOOTPATHS
ROADS

N
W · E
S

ROUTE SUMMARY

MAP: OS Outdoor Leisure Map 6

START: Old station car park, Coniston, GR 300976

DISTANCE: Approximately 6 miles (9.5km)

TIME: 4 – 4½ hours

DIFFICULTY: High-level route. One very steep descent

ROUTE DIRECTION

To reach the start of the walk, turn off the main road in Coniston village at the sign 'Footpath Old Man, Walna Scar and Seathwaite'. The sign points towards Station Road. Near the top of the road turn left to the old station car park.

1 Return to Station Road and turn left up the tarmac lane.

2 The lane climbs steeply, then levels and curves sharply to the right where a track branches off it to the left. Continue along the lane, following the sign for 'Walna Scar, Coniston Old Man'.

3 The lane ends at a car park where the path splits three ways. Turn right (north-west) on the track signposted 'Public footpath Coniston Old Man via Low Water'.

4 Stay on the main track where another branches to the left, and follow it to a ridge overlooking the quarry.

5 A major track cuts across the way here; turn left on this up the fellside.

6 Stay on this track all the way up to Low Water, ignoring any branches you see to the left.

7 From Low Water, a clear path continues up to the summit of the Old Man. Along the way two minor paths branch first to the right and then to the left. Go past both of them and stay on the main path.

8 From the summit, continue to the north along the narrow plateau and bear right where the path forks, keeping Low Water's combe to your right.

9 Follow the series of cairns down to Levers Hawse.

10 At the deepest part of the Hawse, where the plateau has narrowed into a sharp ridge, a tiny cairn stands on the left of the path. Look to your right (east) here, and you will see a grassy slope. Take a few steps down the slope and you will see another small cairn that marks the beginning of the path down to the tarn.

11 On nearing the tarn, the path crosses an inflow stream. Cross the stream and then leave the main path, following the stream down to the shore.

12 Here, another path follows the western shore. Before reaching the dam and weir, it drops down to the right and then approaches the outflow stream.

13 Cross the stream on the rocks and boulders and then turn right, heading towards the quarry.

14 Above the quarry, the main track curves sharply to the right where another branches left (in effect straight on) through two gateposts. Stay on the main track here and go down into the quarry.

15 The track leads through the quarry and then down to the Coppermines Heritage Centre and youth hostel.

16 Continue from there and then turn right over the stone bridge. Soon you will come to some farm buildings and then arrive at some cottages and the Sun Hotel.

17 Turn right on the road in front of the hotel, right again at the facing old well, and then follow the road round to the left to return to the old station car park.

CHAPTER 13

BLIND TARN, GOAT'S WATER & SEATHWAITE TARN

Dunnerdale in late summer, looking towards the eastern slopes of Harter Fell

A valley stretches over 10 miles (16km) from Cockley Beck, near Wrynose Bottom, to Duddon Sands and the sea. It is sheltered to the east by a mountain chain which begins at Wetherlam, then continues through the Coniston Fells to White Maiden, and ends at the Dunnerdale Fells. On the western side, another chain runs southwards from Harter Fell to Great Worm Crag, then on through the Ulpha and Thwaites Fells. The valley is named Dunnerdale, and its beauty is one of Lakeland's best-kept secrets. The River Duddon flows through the fertile valley basin, flanked by forests and high crags. A number of small settlements and farmhouses are dotted along its course, disturbed only by the few tourists who have been fortunate enough to pass this way. The absence of a lake is the main reason for Dunnerdale's lack of visitors, plus the fact that it does not lie on the route to any well-known attractions.

Little has been written about the valley, but wherever mention is made, it usually refers to one Robert Walker of Seathwaite hamlet. Born in 1710, 'wonderful Walker' became one of the Lake District's greatest folk heroes, renowned for his inexhaustible energy and selfless works. Officially recognised as the parish cleric, he also acted as the local physician and lawyer. At other times he could be found teaching at the school, working in the forests, planting crops, tending to sheep on the fells, repairing clothes and spinning cotton. Only after his wife died in 1800 did his spirit weaken, and he followed her two years later, aged ninety two.

Our walk begins 1 mile (1.5km) from Seathwaite and leads to three of Lakeland's finest tarns. The distance covered is 6½ miles, (10.5km) requiring about four hours walking time. Inexperienced walkers might have some difficulty on two of the sections where the route leaves recognised footpaths, but otherwise the going is relatively easy.

THE WALK

The journey starts on an ancient thoroughfare known as the Walna Scar Road, which links Dunnerdale with Coniston. Over much of its course, this is a 'road' only in name, and it is a source of great frustration for mountain bikers, who expect to be able to ride over it. But for walkers, the track is an absolute delight. At the outset, we branch away up the fellside, where another track comes down from Seathwaite Tarn, marking the route of our eventual return.

Our track climbs through open fellsides towards the ridge between Brown Pike and White Maiden. Harter Fell dominates the valley's closest peaks to the rear, and then the Scafell range comes

Above: Dawn above Blind Tarn. The first snows of winter on Brown Pike, with Coniston Water shrouded in mist

into view in the distance. As more height is gained, the view extends way beyond Dunnerdale to the far western peaks, but at the top of the rise even this magnificent panorama pales into insignificance. To the east and south, the land falls over Torver High Common to Coniston Water and the coast. Suddenly the facing aspect of ridges and peaks disappears, and our vision is filled by light, air and the shimmering sea. It is a spectacular transformation, and a rich reward for the long ascent from Dunnerdale.

The path begins its descent to Coniston, passing a remarkably well-preserved stone shelter. Soon, we branch away from Walna Scar over a narrow ledge on the steep mountainside. The Old Man of Coniston comes into view, its slopes leading down to the lake through Little Arrow Moor.

Since the days when the earliest settlers built their burial mounds and cairns here, the whole area has been the subject of outlandish tales. In common with other regions throughout the world with ancient monuments and earthworks, Little Arrow Moor and

the Torver Commons are associated with a much more modern phenomenon: unidentified flying objects. In 1954, two local boys were on Little Arrow Moor when they saw an 'aircraft' manoeuvring at speeds and trajectories that conventional machines could not possibly achieve. A photograph was taken, and promptly developed by a reputable Coniston laboratory, revealing a classic 'flying saucer' image. Newspapers published the picture, and despite exhaustive interrogation and research, nothing was ever found to suggest that it was a hoax.

With the moors and wide-open spaces beneath us, the path follows the contour of Brown Pike, and then enters an area of shattered rocks and slates that mark the site of abandoned quarry workings. We pass a cluster of old stone huts, and then a jewel appears at our feet, tucked into a small pocket on the steep mountainside. Of all the high Lakeland tarns, this one comes as the greatest surprise. There is nothing to betray its presence to observers on lower ground: no outlet stream, or obvious mountain combe, hence its name, Blind Tarn.

A narrow ledge and shallow moraine hold the tarn in place at an altitude of 1,870ft (570m). On the southern side, a steep slope leads to the summit of Brown Pike, then curves to the north-west and the summit of Buck Pike. Elsewhere, the surroundings consist of the narrow band of moraine, after which there is only sky. This wide open aspect gives the tarn a bright, spacious outlook and a giddy sense of height. A few paces across the moraine are all that is required to look out over Coniston Water and the southern lowlands, with the Old Man dominating the scene to the north-east.

Although the tarn is small, with a diameter of about 100yd (30m), it holds a large number of trout and char. Throughout the daylight hours, their surface ripples never seem to end. I am told that the volcanic rock of the area should make the water too acid for fish to thrive, but they succeed nevertheless. The shoreline is easily

Above: Morning sunshine on Goat's Water and Dow Crag. Looking south towards the sea from Goat's Hawse

accessible all the way around, even beneath the steep slopes, an open invitation to test the beautifully clear water, which reaches a maximum depth of around 20ft (6m).

In summer, the sun is high enough to keep the tarn in direct light for much of the day. At other times of the year it is better to come here in the mornings, before Brown Pike casts a shadow across the surface. But whenever one chooses to visit, there is an almost impertinent charm about Blind Tarn, as it rests here in the most unexpected of locations.

Our route descends steeply to the north-east on grassy slopes dotted with enormous boulders, heading for the combe between the Old Man and Dow Crag. The mountains' silence is broken as Goat's Water's outflow stream draws near, crashing down over its rocky bed. Then a short ascent alongside the beck leads into the awesomely rugged combe, and reveals the tarn at an altitude of 1,645ft (501m).

Boulders and rocks are everywhere around Goat's Water: on the steep mountain sides, on the shore and particularly around the outflow. Invariably, the eye is drawn to the western side, where the spectacular heights of Dow Crag reach for the sky. The uppermost ramparts fall in sheer rock faces, divided here and there by deep gullies, and then come down to the water's edge through precipitous screes and fallen boulders. The tarn is held in place by these rock falls, and fed by a stream that comes in from the north.

Normally, the back wall of a combe tarn is the highest part of the surroundings, roughly opposite the outflow. But here, Dow Crag and the Old Man lie to the sides, on the west and east respectively. At the northern end the ground is lower, formed by Goat's Hawse, a col that links the two dominant mountains. At the southern end the land opens, offering a distant view of the sea. The best time to come here is before noon, when Dow Crag is still in direct sunlight and the tarn is free of shadow cast by the Old Man. Despite the hard,

rocky environment and steep screes, Goat's Water's shoreline is accessible practically all the way around. It measures approximately 350yd (320m) from north to south, and 140yd (130m) at the widest point. Over 40ft (12m) deep, the water is clean, cold and sharply invigorating.

Trout and char have been found here as long as anyone can remember, but as with all the tarns, the origin of the fish is unknown. Some tarns have certainly been stocked over the centuries, but it is posible that Goat's Water and other remote tarns acquired their fish by natural means, possibly by eggs attached to wading birds.

For those walkers who wish to spend some time exploring the nooks and crannies of this wild place, a famous scramble leads through one of the gullies to the summit of Dow Crag. But be warned: that large blue chest at the top of the scree contains mountain rescue equipment which is regularly put to use. A safer way to enjoy the view from Dow Crag is to detour at the top of Goat's Hawse, the next objective of our route.

At the col, we leave well-trodden paths and descend over a steep, grassy slope toward the small valley at the northern tip of Seathwaite Tarn. Few people venture into this sheltered hollow, so the solitary path is very difficult to follow. The chosen route therefore follows a stream and then turns to the west, following the low contours of the hillside. Seathwaite Tarn's northern tip comes into view, where Raven Nest How guards the entrance to the valley.

A wonderful introduction to the tarn is to leave the path where it skirts Raven Nest How, and step onto the pinnacle of this large rock outcrop. The sun arcs across the open southern sky, brightly illuminating the surface and increasing the sense of scale. Nowadays, this is one of the largest tarns in Lakeland, stretching over 1,300yd (1,190m) to the south-east, where a dam holds back the massive bulk of water. It was built by Barrow Corporation and, subsequently passed

The view back to the northern reaches from the dam could not be a greater contrast to the spacious outlook in the south. An enormous ridge formed by Swirl How and Great Carrs towers above the valley head, seeming to bar any exit in that direction.

The main inlet stream comes in from the north-east, with two more falling down from the eastern crags. Tarn Beck escapes through the dam, beginning its long and winding course down to the River Duddon. Seathwaite used to enjoy a reputation as a fine trout water, and there are still many fish in its crystal clear depths. I am told, however, that they do not grow to any great size because of the acidity of the water. The Fresh Water Biological Research Association is currently engaged in an experiment here, adding nutrients to the water in an attempt to increase algae which improve pH levels.

I have often been at this tarn around sunset, and enjoyed watching the colourful reflection of sky and clouds fade gradually on the water, but I have stayed overnight on only one occasion. I find there is something melancholy about the place, a poignancy emphasised by the vast grandeur of this mountain pass. Perhaps it is merely the scale of the surroundings and the lack of visitors that create a feeling of emptiness, for there is much to see and explore, and of special interest are the shapes of the surrounding crags.

The final leg of our route begins by crossing the dam, where the deep water is completely clear to the stony bottom. A long, wide track winds down from here. It is kept in good repair for vehicles which transport men and machinery on annual maintenance trips to the dam. On the descent, Dunnerdale's green basin and woods grow ever larger beyond the sloping moorland and a network of dry stone walls. The peaceful outlook and comfortable track provide a very pleasant, relaxing way to end a memorable day. About thirty minutes after leaving the tarn, the track brings us back to the Walna Scar Road, exactly at our starting point.

into the hands of North West Water. But it was already a sizeable tarn before the dam's construction raised the water level to a maximum depth approaching 100ft (30m), and increased the distance between the western and eastern shore to around 400yd (370m).

On the eastern side, the land comes down from Dow Crag in a series of crags which fall steeply into the water, interspersed by sections with gentler gradients that offer more comfortable access to the shore. To the north-west, the slope is less severe immediately around the tarn, then rises sharply to Grey Friar. About half way down the western side, a rock island lies a few yards offshore, next to the spot where the surrounding ground falls away and the dam begins.

Above: Seathwaite Tarn reflects the fading light of a September day.
Viewed from beneath Raven Nest How

ROUTE DIRECTIONS

One mile north of Seathwaite hamlet in Dunnerdale, a lane branches off the main road, heading to the east and signposted 'Coniston via Walna Scar. Unfit for motors'. Go down the lane and carry straight on where a branch goes to the left. Near the end of the lane, go through the farm gate and then park at the small spaces 50yd (45m) further on, where the lane effectively ends.

1 A wide track continues from here, bearing left over a bridge, but our route is to the right, following the footpath sign-posted 'Public Bridleway Walna Scar'. This leads all the way to the top of the facing ridge.

2 At the top, carry straight on at a cross-path, heading down towards Coniston Water. Watch for a stone shelter on your left, and then a small cairn on your right.

3 About 20yd (18m) further down from the cairn, a grassy path branches left, up the hillside. Follow it until you reach the first of the abandoned quarry buildings, where it disappears.

4 Carry straight on in the same direction, two paces to the right of the first stone hut.

5 After passing through the cluster of huts, the path becomes obvious and curves sharply to the right. Branch off to the left here, on a minor path which leads down to Blind Tarn.

6 To leave the tarn, walk into the shallowest part of the moraine above the eastern shore until you can see the point where the lower slope of the Old Man of Coniston appears to meet the lake. Head directly towards that point, keeping a rock-filled gully to your left.

7 Carry on towards the same point when the descent comes to a shallow gully, and you will arrive at a grassy ledge that leads down to your left. Follow it and then continue to the north, wherever you feel comfortable. The general direction is towards the combe between Dow Crag and the Old Man.

8 Before you arrive at Goat's Water's outflow beck, you might see a sheep trod that leads up to the tarn. If so, stay on it. If not, once you come to the beck, follow it upstream and look to your left. The sheep trod lies about 10yd (9m) to the left of the beck.

9 When the tarn comes into view, cross the beck to join the bridleway that follows the eastern shore and then rises up the col (Goat's Hawse) at the northern end.

10 At the top of the col, go straight across the main path that cuts across your way, and begin to descend, heading north-wards.

11 At this point a faint track leads down into the valley, bearing slightly to your right. It passes to the right of a long gully and stream. In order to avoid confusion at the bottom of the descent, leave the path now and go down the grassy slope, keeping the gully and stream to your right.

12 As you continue to descend, bear slightly to your left and you will see another gully and stream. Continue your descent in between the two gullies.

13 As you approach the bottom of the descent, look out for a tiny cairn on the opposite side of the stream on your left (west). It stands about 300yd (270m) from the valley basin. When you see it, cross the stream, and you will see a track that heads due west and follows the contour of the hillside.

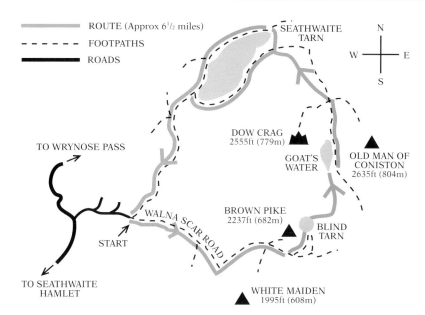

14 On nearing Seathwaite Tarn, there is a choice of two routes. Staying on the present path will lead along the tarn's undulating and rocky eastern shore. The path along the western shore is more comfortable, but to reach it entails crossing the inflow beck. This can be difficult at times, particularly after rainfall.

15 Both paths converge at the tarn's south-western tip, beyond the dam. Follow the wide track that leads to the south-west from here, and stay on it where a path branches to the right.

16 After thirty minutes the track leads back to your starting point.

ROUTE SUMMARY

MAP:	OS Outdoor Leisure Map 6
START:	Walna Scar Road, Dunnerdale, GR 238968
DISTANCE:	Approximately 6½ miles (10.5km)
TIME:	4 – 4½ hours
DIFFICULTY:	Leaves recognised footpaths on two sections, needs concentration

CHAPTER 14

ESKDALE

A busy autumn afternoon at Dalegarth Station, as 'Little Ratty' prepares to leave for the coast

Eskdale is one of the few major Lakeland valleys without a lake. From the head at Hard Knott, it rolls down to the coast near Ravenglass, covering a distance of about 10 miles (16km). Drainage is provided by the River Esk, which issues from a mountainous region around Crinkle Crags and Bow Fell, then meanders through lush meadows flanked by deciduous woods and high fells. The woodland and greenery more than compensate for the lack of a lake, and Eskdale is ranked with Borrowdale and Dunnerdale as the most sublime of Lakeland districts.

By road, access to the valley's lower reaches is possible only from the coastal areas or Dunnerdale. At the head of Eskdale, the solitary entry or exit is by way of Hardknott Pass. This narrow, precipitous thoroughfare with many twists and turns, is quite an attraction in itself. The site of a Roman fort lies on a rocky spur on the western side of the pass. From here there are views of the highest mountains in Lakeland to the east, while to the west Eskdale's full course can be seen all the way to the coast. A great deal of restoration has been carried out at the stone-built fort. Now it stands as one of England's finest examples of a second century military stronghold.

Scenic grandeur notwithstanding, Eskdale's principal attraction is the Ravenglass and Eskdale railway. Justifiably publicised as 'the most beautiful train journey in England', this miniature railway is great fun for all the family.

Opened in 1875 by the Whitehaven Mining Company, it was originally a 3ft gauge track, built to transport iron ore down to the main coastal railway. A passenger service was quickly introduced, but iron ore production waned and the future of the railway was in jeopardy. Granite quarries were opened in an attempt to boost trade, but the line was forced to close in 1913. Salvation came the following year in the form of Mr Basset-Lowke, a well-known model maker. He relaid the line in 15in gauge, a novelty which increased public interest and enabled the service to prosper until 1953 when the quarries closed.

Although much improved, the tourist trade at the time was not sufficient in itself to support the line. In 1960 it was sold by auction to a group of enthusiasts who subsequently passed it on, into the capable hands of the present operators. With support from a preservation society, the railway grew ever more successful and is now one of north-west England's premier tourist attractions. Open all year, it runs from Dalegarth in the heart of Eskdale for a distance of 7 miles (11km). Stops are made along the way at five tiny rural stations, and it ends at Ravenglass, where visitors can delve into history at the railway museum. Some train carriages are roofed, others are open to take full advantage of good weather. Dalegarth Station has a large car park with a picnic area, where you can await the trains.

BURNMOOR AND BLEA TARNS (ESKDALE)

This route is approximately 5$\frac{1}{2}$ miles (9km) long and requires only two and a half hours' walking time. Along the first section approaching Eskdale Moor, the path has a rather awkward stretch with stones and rocks underfoot, but this passes quickly. Closer to Burnmoor Tarn it is necessary to watch for marshy patches along the way, but apart from that there are no difficulties. If you feel that the distance is within your capabilities, then have no qualms about tiring climbs. For the most part height is gained gently until you reach Blea Tarn. After that there comes a steep but comfortable descent.

The walk begins at Dalegarth Station car park, and heads down the valley road where Harter Fell crowns the eastern skyline. On the far side of the hamlet of Boot an old pack-horse bridge crosses Burnmoor Tarn's outflow Whillan Beck. Immediately beyond this stands a 600 year old corn mill that has been restored to working order and is open to visitors. As the route gently rises on a rocky bridleway, a view of Eskdale with its eastern fells opens slowly to the rear. Whillan Beck cascades down through a wooded gorge on the right, and beyond stands the pointed aspect of Great Barrow.

After a series of farm gates, the path passes out onto open moorland and becomes much easier underfoot. Eskdale is left behind as we travel on an old route linking it with Wasdale. Soon we are far out onto Eskdale Moor, an area steeped in the history of ancient peoples. This is the only Lakeland path I know that can generate a feeling of loneliness. Many myths and legends are told about the Lake District, and most should be taken with a pinch of salt. But this track is renowned for a tale which fits the surroundings so well that I feel there must be some truth in it.

In the days before Wasdale church was built, coffins were carried on horseback over the moor for burial at Boot. A young man's funeral procession was heading that way through mist and rain when the coffin-bearing horse bolted and was lost. Distraught at the news that her son would not be buried in consecrated ground, his mother subsequently died of a broken heart. Her own cortège set out across the moor, once again in mist, but this time with snow on the ground. Again, the horse bolted taking the old woman's corpse with it. Searchers were able to follow some tracks in the snow, and these eventually led to a thin, shivering creature. It was the horse with the son's coffin. He was therefore buried, but the mother's horse and coffin were never found. Perhaps you might care to bear this in mind if you head towards Burnmoor on a misty day.

As we approach the tarn, Illgill Head appears over the highest point of the moor to the left. Ahead and to the right Scafell looms ever larger, then Red Pike, Yewbarrow and Kirk Fell rise above the distant skyline above Wasdale Head. Finally, the vast expanse of Burnmoor Tarn lies beneath us.

The tarn occupies a large hollow set in a wide enclave between

Eskdale Fell, Scafell and Illgill Head, at an altitude of 830ft (253m). Scafell and Illgill Head are well known for their rugged, precipitous slopes and broken crags. But Scafell's harsher character is confined to its northern and eastern sides while Illgill Head is famous for the screes that plunge to the west into Wast Water. Both peaks present kindlier faces to Burnmoor, rolling down to the tarn through long, gentle slopes. The only steep or craggy aspect is on Eskdale Fell's western slope.

Large quantities of moraine between Eskdale Moor and Miterdale hold the great weight of water at its southern end. An outflow in the north-western corner joins forces with Hardrigg Gill, which comes down from Scafell and then proceeds to the south. Streams feed in from a col to the north, above which Yewbarrow, Kirk Fell and Great Gable provide a contrast to the soft outlines of the tarn's immediate surroundings. Grass and bracken cover the gentle slopes now, where once there was forest, and nothing interrupts the unbroken sweep of the hillsides.

After deforestation the area was fertile for some time, and provided a home for a sizeable population. Numerous stone circles can be found hereabouts and the name Burnmoor itself gives a clue to the history. It is thought to be derived from an Old English word referring to 'borrans' or burial mounds on the moors. Above the tarn's northern shore lie the ruins of a Celtic fort marked on maps as Maiden Castle. Other stone constructions around Burnmoor date back to the Bronze Age.

This is one of Lakeland's largest tarns. Its relatively smooth outlines measure approximately 920yd by 480yd (840m by 440m) and the water reaches a maximum depth of over 40ft (12m). The grassy shore is accessible all the way around, although it is a little marshy here and there. Bathers will probably find the south-eastern section to their liking, as it is along there that the water becomes deep quickly. However, Burnmoor's wide open location is usually windswept and

cool. Moreover, no great effort is required to reach it, so walkers do not work up the kind of lather that can make some tarns appear like an oasis in a desert, and a swim an absolute must. Only on exceptionally warm days, therefore, are you likely to be tempted.

This is more than compensated for, however, by the quality and quantity of Burnmoor's fish. Brown trout, perch, pike and eels are abundant, the shallow water around the northern shore providing the richest harvest. One of the local farmers tows fishing boats up here, complete with sonar equipment. On one occasion I could hear the anglers gasping in astonishment at the size of the shoals they were locating.

On Ordnance Survey maps, there is a small square near the south-eastern shore which is clearly marked as Burnmoor Lodge. For many people this lodge is shrouded in mystery. It is a well-maintained building, about the size of a modern semi-detached house. There is a walled enclosure immediately in front of it and a biblical plaque is fixed to the eastern wall of the house, on the side that most visitors first approach. Because of its isolation, the lodge is conspicuous from all angles around Burnmoor, and in common with most other visitors, I have often wondered why such a lonely building is so obviously well maintained and yet boarded shut, seemingly deserted. My enquiries about its owner have met with explanations varying from a strange religious sect to a Chinese lady from Manchester. I know that many other theories have been circulated, but on my latest visit I discovered the truth.

Burnmoor Lodge definitely is not abandoned. The house and enclosure are the property of a gentleman from Yorkshire who keeps it in good repair for the benefit of family and friends. Unfortunately, it transpires that some passers-by have allowed their curiosity to get the better of them and the lodge has suffered occasional break-ins. Now the owner has been forced to remove any valuables, bringing

Right: A late autumn afternoon at Burnmoor Tarn. The lodge can be seen beneath Eskdale Fell, with Scafell in the distance

everything he needs for his visits from home. This information came from friends of his who were quietly enjoying their retreat until my intrusion one fine day in August. In thanks to them, and on behalf of the owner, I ask that all walkers keep a respectful distance.

On leaving Burnmoor our path passes close by the lodge, over the crest of the facing hillside, and then follows the contours of Boat How. The path is dry and grassy, with a view over Eskdale Moor to the high ground around Great Barrow and Eel Tarn. Between Boat How and Miterdalehead Moss the path enters a group of stone circles on Brat's Hill. Many more circles and cairns can be found in the vicinity, testimony to its importance in the distant past. Burials were most certainly carried out here, and easy access from Eskdale, Miterdale and Wasdale would have made it a logical meeting place. There are wide horizons to east and west, suggesting that the stones could have been aligned with heavenly bodies. It is well known that similar circles around the country were constructed in this way, and served as calendars. In more recent times, dales folk gathered here to celebrate the Feast of Beltane. On May nights great fires would be lit to see off the last vestiges of winter.

A little further along the way a view of Eskdale unfolds fleetingly until the path enters a section of undulating ground and rocky knolls. It then continues down to the southernmost tip of the long ridge formed by Eskdale Moor and Miterdalehead Moss. There Blea Tarn sits snugly above Eskdale at an altitude of 700ft (213m), and in many ways this is the highlight of our route. It is held on two sides by moraine and rock outcrops which open out to the south-west, facing the sea. The outflow beck wanders this way and then falls sharply down the end of the ridge to join the River Esk. On the northern side Bleatarn Hill rises above the shore, offering an extensive view. To the east, beyond Eskdale's unseen basin, Hesk Fell and Ulpha Fell point the way into the heart of Lakeland's mountains, and to the

south, Birkby Fell sweeps down to the coast. Moving steadily westwards, our line of sight passes over flat lands and fields around the estuary. Then comes Muncaster Fell, breaking the broad sweep of the sea on the horizon. In late autumn and winter the sun sets along that horizon and Blea Tarn shimmers in its glow. The shore is basically oval-shaped, with occasional rocky outcrops breaking the lines. It measures roughly 280yd (260m) from south-west to north-east and 150yd (140m) across. The water here is always crystal clear and contains some good trout and perch. It is very difficult to approach the shore on the western side because of the relatively steep, bracken-covered slope, but elsewhere the approach is easy on firm, dry ground.

The open southern aspect and low surround fill Blea Tarn's hollow with air, light and a warm welcome. A particularly good spot from which to savour the wholesome atmosphere and gaze out over the sea is around the outflow, and although the journey is almost over, Blea Tarn is nevertheless a wonderful place to camp. There are many comfortable locations around the shore, and rocky outcrops within the containing moraine provide shelter if necessary.

There are two more tarns on the tip of this ridge: Siney Tarn and Blind Tarn. Both are tiny and mostly overgrown with reeds, but the sea views from them are worth a five-minute detour. Immediately after leaving Blea Tarn, the path zigzags down Hollinghead Bank. It comes as a surprise to see Eskdale so far below, as the path from it did not seem to climb this high. Now the views are magnificent, covering the full course of the valley from the Hardknott Pass to the sea. To the east, the horizon is filled by the smooth outlines of Ulpha and Hesk Fells, which fall to the verdant pastures of the valley. Large areas of woodland and small copses are seen decorating slopes and fields as we head back to Dalegarth, passing over the miniature railway on the way. After crossing the line, a two-minute walk along the valley road brings us back to the station.

Left: Autumn tints around Blea Tarn, looking south towards the coast

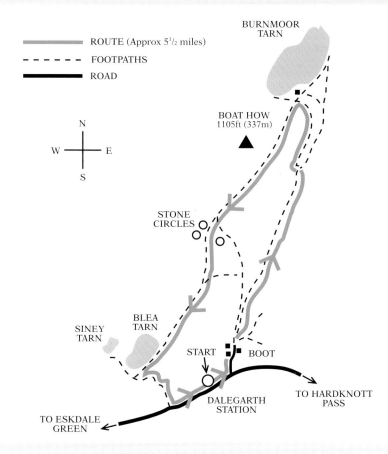

Legend:
- ROUTE (Approx 5½ miles)
- FOOTPATHS
- ROAD

N W E S

BURNMOOR TARN

BOAT HOW
1105ft (337m)

STONE CIRCLES

BLEA TARN

SINEY TARN

START

BOOT

DALEGARTH STATION

TO HARDKNOTT PASS

TO ESKDALE GREEN

ROUTE DIRECTIONS

1 From Dalegarth Station turn left on the road and then left again into Boot.

2 Go straight through the hamlet and then follow the sign 'Public Bridleway Burnmoor Tarn, Wasdale Head', This leads over a stone bridge to a gate.

3 Go through the gate and turn right at the 'Bridleway' sign.

4 Shortly after this, the path forks. Turn right here, and go through another gate. After a series of farm gates, the path leads out onto open moorland.

5 Along the way to Burnmoor Tarn you might see a faint fork in the path. If you do, it is better to take the left branch as this leads more directly to the tarn's shore. However, it is of no great importance, as both paths lead to Burnmoor.

6 To leave the tarn, go back past Burnmoor Lodge, heading south-west on the highest path you see. This leads to a cross-path and over the crest of the hill. To be certain of taking the correct route, go to the path that runs past the back wall of the lodge. From there, follow the path heading to where you first arrived above the tarn.

7 At the cross-path, turn sharp right up the hillside.

8 After passing the highest point of Boat How on your right, the main path bears left at a fork, which is not marked on Ordnance Survey maps. Ignore the left branch and carry straight on to the stone circles.

9 Here you will see the path continuing to the left of two circles and to the right of a third, after which it forks again. Take the right branch, following the higher ground.

10 There are many narrow tracks around here that are not marked on maps. Continue to bear right at every fork and cross-path you see.

11 Eventually you will see a major path coming up from Eskdale to join your path from the left, at a point marked by a disused mine shaft. Carry straight on here.

12 The path forks again within some rocky knolls, the right branch climbing a knoll and the left leading down over grass. Either one can be taken, as they converge before reaching Blea Tarn.

13 Follow the path along Blea Tarn's eastern shore and then take the left branch at the south-eastern corner. This leads down the fellside towards Eskdale, eventually passing over the miniature railway.

14 Immediately after crossing the line turn left on the road back to Dalegarth Station.

ROUTE SUMMARY

MAP: OS Outdoor Leisure Map 6

START: Dalegarth Station, Eskdale, GR 173007

DISTANCE: Approximately 5½ miles (9km)

TIME: 2¼ - 2¾ hours

DIFFICULTY: None

Left: September in Eskdale. Viewed from the route on Hollinghead Bank, looking east towards the Hardknott Pass

STONY AND EEL TARNS

This second walk from Eskdale covers a distance of approximately 3 miles (5km) and can be accomplished in one and a half hours. There is little climbing to do, and the highest point of the route, Stony Tarn, can be reached in twenty minutes by an experienced walker. However, that is not to say that this is an easy stroll. The route up to Stony Tarn is clear initially, but then becomes very difficult to see. Between Stony and Eel Tarns the path is virtually non-existent, although there is a right of way. It is a very good route to test map-reading and compass skills without having to travel far from safety – ideal perhaps for school parties or those who enjoy exploring knolls and hollows.

The Woolpack Inn is a little further up the valley road from Dalegarth Station, heading towards the Hardknott Pass. A path leads up from a farmyard behind the inn. The clear grassy track rises up through bracken, with Eskdale falling away to the right. Then it leads into a maze of knolls and rock outcrops, where it disappears intermittently. This is obviously a little-used path, a place where walkers are left very much to their own devices. It can be pleasant to wander here, exploring each new close horizon or hollow, but it can be disorientating, as it is very easy to 'recognise' an area that you have not actually seen before.

The route rises over several areas of grass, moss and bogs that form steps up to a large, rocky protuberance known as Peelplace Noddle. Between this and another crag, a narrow passage allows Stony Tarn's outflow to escape. We follow the passage and then the course of the stream as the ground opens to reveal the tarn.

It rests in a bowl formed by rocky hillsides and projecting crags at an altitude of 975ft (297m). A glance at its clear, shallow water reveals the stony bed after which the tarn was named. Unfortunately, the shallow water means that fish cannot survive here, as there is insufficient protection from the sun's rays. Swimming is possible however, and the south-western bearing of the sheltered hollow makes it a warm place to bathe. High ground above the southern and eastern shores presents a colourful and varied face. Hard, dark rocks contrast with thick grasses and stunted heather while bracken presents varying hues throughout the year, all of which provides a background for the light green of the mosses and grass around the waterside.

A single inlet stream comes down from Cat Cove, entering the tarn at the north-western corner of its roughly pear-shaped shoreline, which measures approximately 200yd (180m) in length from south-west to north-east and 110yd (100m) at the widest point. The south-eastern side, with a couple of promontories and bays, is the most interesting. There is nothing to prevent access to the water at any point, and the flat, grassy land around the waterside offers many comfortable sites for picnickers or campers.

Understandably, Stony Tarn has a reputation for being difficult to find. It lies well away from the main walking routes, and as you will already have discovered, there are no clear paths to or from it. Because of this, it is one of the least visited tarns that I know. I have been here on at least six occasions but have yet to see another person. Once I noticed a tent pitched snugly between some rocky outcrops near the southern shore, but no sign of the owners. It is almost certain therefore that you will have the place to yourself – a mouth-watering prospect. Take the time to explore the surrounding ridge; there is a rewarding view of the Scafell range to the north, and a chance to watch the sun arc slowly over the sea to the south-west.

The route from here to Eel Tarn is almost unmarked. A path appears to head towards it from Stony Tarn's outflow, but this becomes unclear until very close to Eel Tarn. It is much simpler to go to the enclosing ridge at the south-west of Stony Tarn. Here you can look down over Eskdale Moor and see Eel Tarn beneath you. After passing across and around various patches of grass and marsh, the way leads through a gully, and then Eel Tarn appears ahead and below.

It has a bright and spacious setting on a shelf within rocky hills. Its position at the edge of the fell, above Whillan Beck and Eskdale Moor, provides views to the north-west, where the smooth face of Illgill Head climbs above the moor, and Yewbarrow is seen in the distance beyond Wast Water. On the other sides the ground is a little too high to extend the panorama.

Eel Tarn lies at an altitude of 700ft (213m), and has an overall oval shape which tapers off to a point at the north-western corner. From here, the outflow begins its descent towards Whillan Beck. It is around this part of the shore that access to the water is easiest. Elsewhere, the open ground mainly consists of mosses and marsh. Large areas of reeds are further barriers. The tarn measures approximately 220yd (200m) from north-west to south-east and 110yd (100m) across. The water is mainly shallow, and is sprinkled here and there with lilies. There are a good number of trout here, but they are generally small

Despite its difficult shoreline, Eel Tarn is a cheerful and colourful spot. It is very pleasant to while away some time on the high knoll at the northern end, from where we can sit looking across the tarn or over the moor. The best camping is also around this knoll.

Surprisingly, the tarn's name has nothing to do with eels. There are two possible derivations, but since one can be applied only to something steep or precipitous, which Eel Tarn patently is not, we can assume that it comes from an old Norse word that translates as

'evil'. It is believed that it is so called because of the phenomenon known as will-o'-the-wisp. Methane gas sometimes accumulates in pockets above marshland, creating a ghostly effect as it moves in the breeze. The large number of marshes here would provide ample opportunity for sightings of the phenomenon, and thus explain the tarn's unflattering name.

A very clear path leads away from the tarn as we head back to Eskdale. The descent winds through a number of small granite crags before coming back to the farmyard behind the Woolpack Inn.

Above: Stony Tarn lies peacefully beneath a September sky.
Looking south-west towards the coast

Overleaf: The end of an autumn day at Eel Tarn

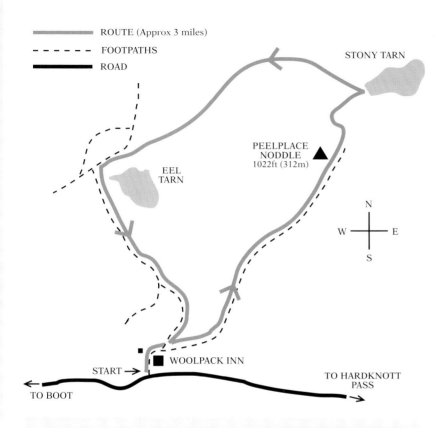

ROUTE DIRECTIONS

1 A lane goes off the main valley road, on the opposite (eastern) side of the Woolpack Inn from its car park. At the entrance is a sign marked 'Public Footpath Burnmoor/Wasdale Head'. Follow in the direction of the sign and go straight across the cross-track amongst the farm buildings. In the farmyard behind the cottages you will see a narrow path that climbs the hillside.

2 Follow the path up to a gate, after which it forks and then reconverges.

3 At a second fork take the right branch, on the grass track through the bracken. This path passes close to the wall on your right. The left branch is bordered by a line of stones and marks the way you will return at the end of the walk.

4 A few minutes into the ascent, the path becomes unclear and only appears intermittently from this point up to Stony Tarn. Remember that your general direction is north-north-east. Various patches of marsh and a succession of gullies lie ahead.

5 From the point where the path becomes unclear, carry on upwards at all times, keeping to as straight a line as possible through the gullies, and you will reach a section where the path is clear.

6 This leads up to a flat, grassy area to the right, with higher ground to the left. About 100yd (90m) ahead and to the right is a short waterfall.

7 As the path follows the margin between the flat area and the higher knoll, keep looking to your left and you will see a clear branch going to the left, up the rise. Follow it to a gully and Stony Tarn's outflow beck.

8 The path peters out once more, but follow the beck upstream to arrive at Stony Tarn.

9 To leave the tarn, go to the point of the shoreline where the outflow begins. Look to the west (slightly to your right), and you will see a faint path leading to higher ground. Take this up to the series of small outcrops ahead of you.

10 The furthest outcrop or pinnacle on your left provides a view of Eel Tarn. Take a compass bearing (the heading is southwest), for the tarn is not visible all the way down.

11 Now, simply head straight for the tarn, taking whatever route you find most comfortable.

12 A red/amber patch of wetland, about 50yd (45m) in diameter, lies across the way. Skirt round this to your left.

13 A faint track can now be seen running down to a wide gully. Follow it and Eel Tarn will reappear.

14 Carry on down towards the tarn. Stay on the path that passes around the shore to the right (the north). This continues around the tarn, turning to the south.

15 The path is very clear at the tarn, and remains so until you reach what looks like a fork. Bear left over the wet, peaty section and once again the path becomes clear.

16 When you arrive at a gate and stile, do not pass through the gate, but bear left following the sign for the Woolpack Inn. A couple of minutes later, the path re-enters the farmyard behind the inn.

ROUTE SUMMARY

MAP: OS Outdoor Leisure Map 6

START: Woolpack Inn, Eskdale, GR 190010

DISTANCE: Approximately 3 miles (5km)

TIME: 1¼ – 1¾ hours

DIFFICULTY: Some marshy ground. Paths difficult to follow

CHAPTER 15

SCOAT TARN

The tarn that got away: Low Tarn, with Yewbarrow and the distant Scafells

Wasdale is situated in the far west of the Lake District. By road it can only be approached from the coastal area or from the south-west. Neither route gives any hint of the sudden, dramatic changes in landscape that occur between the entrance to the valley and its head. From inauspicious beginnings in relatively low arable land, it narrows between high ground at the southern reaches of Wast Water and continues into a rugged mountainous region. A road follows the lake shore for about 3 miles (5km) and then carries on a short distance to Wasdale Head hamlet. Here motorists can travel no further, their way blocked by the tallest mountain range in Lakeland. The Scafells, Lingmell, Great Gable, Kirk Fell, Red Pike and Yewbarrow encircle the hamlet and it is owing to their presence that Wasdale Head is recognised as the birthplace of modern British rock climbing.

It is an area of stark grandeur and record-breaking proportions. The summit of Scafell Pike is the highest point in England, Wast Water is the deepest lake, and hidden in a small copse amongst the dry-stone walls of the fields is St Olaf's, the nation's smallest church. Some of the church's wooden beams are said to have been taken from a Viking long ship.

As one would expect, Wasdale is very popular with the walking and climbing fraternity. But they are as ants in the company of giants, and nothing can challenge the solemn majesty of the surroundings or disturb the serene air. On my first visit to the Lake District as a teenager, I stepped out of the car on Wast Water's shore and realised that for the first time in my life I was listening to utter silence.

The National Trust operates a large, well equipped campsite close to the lake's northern tip, and a very small site can be found next to the Wasdale Head Inn. If you have forgotten any equipment or clothing, a good range is available at the shop in the inn's courtyard. The inn itself is a convivial place and caters for all tastes, offering

Wast Water reflects The Screes and the peaks around Wasdale Head on an idyllic autumn afternoon

accommodation, meals and fine ales. It was built to cater 'for the idiots who walk in the hills' by the first landlord, Will Ritson, and the public bar is named after him. His reason for opening the inn gives an insight into the character of the man. The mountains and all who ventured into them were very close to his heart. Born in 1808, he spent all eighty-two years of his life in Wasdale. A boisterous man by all accounts, given to wrestling and horseplay, he was always ready to entertain visitors with his wit. He became well known as a mountain guide and as an instructor for mountaineers, some of whom grew to eminence in the sport. But Will is most fondly remembered as a teller of tall tales. He dominated the inn's annual 'World Champion Liar' competition for many years until a showdown with a visiting bishop, who claimed never to have told a lie. Naturally, Will resigned his title.

The walk to Scoat Tarn begins and ends on the shore of Wast Water. The journey covers approximately 7½ miles (12km), and requires a minimum of four hours. Some high-level sections are included, and about half the altitude is gained gradually. But the remainder involves three steep ascents, one of which is literally a scramble. Because of this and the distance, I recommend that only experienced walkers should attempt the route.

The walk begins at Overbeck Bridge car park on the north-western shore of Wast Water. The first ½ mile (1km) or so follows the lakeside road opposite screes that plunge 1,800ft (550m) into water. Incredibly, there is a footpath along the foot of the scree that runs the length of Wast Water. On another day you might be tempted to try it out, but if so allow plenty of time. Two sections along it demand complete concentration.

The Scafells, Lingmell and Great Gable dominate the scene to our left and rear, with Yewbarrow and Kirk Fell behind to the right. Soon we take a path away from the lake up through Nether Beck's long gully. Over the first rise of the day, the sound of waterfalls welcomes us to fell country. Moving steadily away from Wasdale the route continues to rise gently. Over to the right a path comes down Yewbarrow's facing ridge, marking the way we will return.

Wild, remote country lies ahead as the path follows Nether Beck upstream. The water flows down through a series of falls and rapids, idling here and there in rock pools. Deep ravines have been carved into the rock in places, and the best of them is tree-lined, marking the spot where we ascend the first of three distinct steps that lie between Wasdale and Scoat Tarn.

Picking our way over rocks and boulders we are soon over the first step and onto a level section. There are more waterfalls ahead, cascading down the second step. The path rises over this step, skirting around Great Lad Crag. On the following level Wasdale disappears to the rear, and the path leads into a corrie formed by Red Pike and Haycock. On the facing mountainside, Scoat Tarn's outflow beck completes our ascent's display of waterfalls. Then we cross two minor streams to arrive at the foot of the mountains. Another 1,400ft (425m) lies between us and the highest point of the route on Red Pike. The ascent to Scoat Tarn accounts for half of that, and can be accomplished in no more than twenty minutes. However, despite the proximity of the tarn, it is doubtful whether you will want to push on to it without taking a break. This corrie high at the head of Nether Beck is just too peaceful and remote to pass straight through. Grassy banks and tinkling water in the lea of high peaks call on those who come here to stay awhile and consider what has already been seen and enjoyed.

Now the first of two major climbs begins, leading to Scoat Tarn. The path rises near the outflow beck and arrives at the tarn's western shore. Will Ritson may have gone, but Wasdale has another modern-day hero, the living legend Joss Naylor, and it was on this spot by the

Left: Scoat Tarn from Red Pike's lower slopes, with Seatallan in the background

139

shore of Scoat Tarn that I first saw him. Joss was twenty-four years old when he entered his first fell race and thirty-one when he first won an event. From then on his achievements grew consistently greater, resulting in the award of an MBE in 1976. He is best known for racing across seventy-two consecutive peaks, climbing a total of 40,000ft (12,000m) over a distance of 108 miles (173km), in under twenty-four hours! Joss also dismissed the Welsh Peaks route, consisting of fourteen peaks, all of which tower above 3,000ft (900m) in four hours, forty-six minutes.

He can still be seen here, running around the mountains with his dogs, as he tends his flocks of sheep. I am sure that they often take advantage of having Scoat Tarn in their range of fells. To those of us who merely walk up here it comes as a great delight to relax by the shores and swim in the cool, clear water. Consider what a pleasure it must be to do the same in the course of a working day.

At 1,975ft (602m), this is one of Lakeland's highest tarns. It is oval and measures 380yd (350m) from north to south and 190yd (170m) from east to west. The name is derived from old Norse and means 'the Tarn by the Projecting Rocky Ridge'. Surprisingly, the surroundings do not fall as steeply to the water as might be expected of a high combe tarn, especially one with such a title. Before the walls slope upwards to Red Pike there are large deposits of massive boulders piled on the north-eastern shore, some lying within the water. The north-western side opens a little more, leading up to Haycock, and then flattens out completely to the west and south. When this section is viewed from the opposite end of the tarn, there seems to be very little between the water's surface and a great void, apart from a very narrow margin sparsely occupied by enormous boulders. Above the margin Seatallan's summit peeps into the combe but beyond that there is only sky. This open aspect gives the surface a very bright face and enhances the impression of great height.

The water has a maximum depth approaching 70ft (20m) but I am unable to confirm that it contains any fish, despite its reputation for fine trout. It certainly appears to be a likely habitat and I doubt whether the reluctance of the fish to reveal themselves to me has any great significance. There is a considerable amount of marshy ground around the path on the western side, making it unsuitable for camping. Much better places can be found in the flat south-western area, or a little higher above the south-eastern shore.

Two streams feed in, one from the west and one from the north, the latter being one of the coolest and sweetest I have tasted. The path away from Scoat Tarn follows the course of this stream as we head up towards Red Pike on the second of our journey's steep ascents. The route's scenic section begins now. Looking back over the tarn, the Esk estuary can be seen flowing into the silvery haze of the sea. Sellafield's controversial nuclear plant is also clearly visible on the coast north of the estuary. A little later we arrive on Red Pike at an altitude of 2,710ft (826m). Wast Water reappears to the south and Pillar makes its introduction in the north. The precipitous eastern slope of Red Pike is just feet away from the path and beyond this the view is breathtaking. After Pillar comes Kirk Fell and Great Gable, followed by Great End, Lingmell, the Scafells and, beyond, the sea. Continue along the path and a clockwise gaze reveals Burnmoor Tarn on Eskdale Moor, Eel Tarn, High Birker Tarn, Yewbarrow, a section of Wast Water Screes, Middle Fell, Seatallan, Haycock and Scoat Fell. Of all these, I find the long sweep of Scafell's western slope and the assortment of lesser pinnacles beyond it the most fascinating feature.

A stone and shale path leads from here down to the col on Dore Head. Directly ahead the scramble up Yewbarrow's northern ridge appears daunting, especially if fatigue is starting to take its toll. If the prospect proves too much, there is a quick route back to the car

Left: An autumn evening on Red Pike. Looking towards Dore Head and Yewbarrow, with Scafell beyond Wasdale

very much in evidence now and even Burnmoor Lodge can be seen. The Scafells look even more impressive from here, dominating the eastern skyline. Across the valley immediately to the right, Low Tarn appears in a high shelf on the southern slope of Red Pike. Originally, it was my intention to include this tarn in the route, but no footpaths lead there and I was reluctant to recommend any particular way to it. The land is owned by the National Trust and provides grazing for Joss Naylor's sheep; when I consulted him, he advised me not to include that particular section, as it might lead to erosion of the fellside where none presently exists. In deference to the great man and out of respect for conservation, I have therefore left it out.

In certain conditions, the acoustics of the Lakeland fells can be astonishing. On one visit to Yewbarrow's summit I could see Joss below, collecting his sheep from around the tarn and the lower valley. Every whistle and word echoed around the fells. From distances of up to a mile, even footsteps could be heard when feet or hooves disturbed stones.

As the path continues along Yewbarrow, Wast Water grows ever more prominent and then the full length of the lake is revealed. From this vantage point it appears more like a Norwegian fjord than an English lake. The screes seem to fall vertically into water, and even when the sky is grey the surface retains a shade of blue.

The final leg of our journey descends steeply from here on loose stone and shale. On some sections it is necessary to use hands before the gradient eases and the path becomes firm. Along the way patches of heather add yet more colour to the scene and then we are welcomed back to the valley once more by Nether Beck's serenade. We finish at the rear of Overbeck Bridge car park, and Ritson's Bar awaits us.

park. Simply turn right on the faint track that leads down towards Over Beck, following the lower contours of Yewbarrow. However, that route eliminates the final scenic part of the journey, including a stunning view of Wast Water.

So take a breather and then start the climb up Yewbarrow – it only takes fifteen minutes to arrive on the ridge top. The path runs along the full length of the ridge, descending gently and then rising again to the summit at 2,060ft (628m). Burnmoor Tarn is

Above: The low October sun casts Yewbarrow's shadow across Mosedale.
Looking towards Lingmell and Scafell Pike from Dore Head

ROUTE DIRECTIONS

1 On leaving Overbeck Bridge car park, turn right along the road.

2 About fifteen minutes later you will see a signpost on your right saying 'Public Bridleway', but no track is visible here. Carry on for another 150yd (140m) or thereabouts and keep looking to your right. At the top of a small rise in the road you will see where the path begins and turns sharply right, almost doubling back. This enters the gully alongside Nether Beck and heads upstream with the beck on the right.

3 Where the path becomes unclear, follow the line of cairns. The path disappears intermittently, but if in doubt simply continue upwards following the course of the valley.

4 As you approach the final ascent to Scoat Tarn, the path appears to continue up into a corrie. Look to your right and you will see where our route branches to the right and goes across a stream, heading northeast. If in doubt simply head for the last set of waterfalls that you see.

5 These waterfalls come down from Scoat Tarn, and our path follows them upstream. It is indistinct, but watch for a series of tiny cairns on top of boulders. Again, it does not matter if you miss them, for the beck is on your right and that leads to the tarn.

6 At the tarn the path continues along the western shore. In some areas it becomes very faint and the ground can be marshy. Do not be tempted to follow too closely to the shore or you might find yourself up to your knees in water. Keep to the higher ground on your left, even if that means a little extra climbing.

7 At the north-western tip of the tarn, you will see an inflowing stream. The path up to Red Pike is to the right of this and is just discernible.

8 As you approach the top of the rise the path disappears. Carry straight on up until the ridge-top path cuts across your way.

9 Turn right on this path, over the rocks and up to Red Pike.

10 The path passes slightly to the right of the summit cairn, then becomes unclear again on stony ground. Keep to the left of the southernmost rock outcrop, upon which you will see a cairn. After this the way is clear once more and remains so for the rest of the journey.

11 There now follows a steep descent to Dore Head, which lies at the lowest point of the path between Red Pike and Yewbarrow.

12 If you want to leave the main route when you arrive on Dore Head and take the short cut back, look for a track that branches to the right into the valley of Over Beck. This leads down to the car park.

13 Those wishing to complete the full route should carry on from Dore Head up the ridge of Yewbarrow ahead. Two or three minutes of this ascent is extremely steep, and it is necessary to use hands and feet. The path along the length of Yewbarrow is clearly marked.

14 Now comes the steepest descent of the journey. Where the downward path enters a narrow, scree-filled gully, bear first to the right of the scree, watching for where the path crosses to the other side. A series of tiny cairns guide the way.

15 After the steepest part of the descent, bear left where the path forks and you will come to a stile.

16 Cross the stile and the path leads to the right, following the wall down to a gate. Go through the gate into the car park.

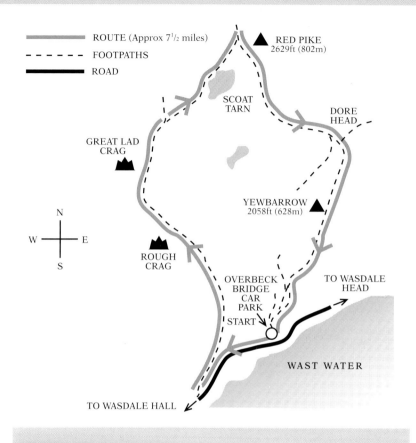

ROUTE (Approx 7½ miles)

FOOTPATHS

ROAD

RED PIKE 2629ft (802m)

SCOAT TARN

DORE HEAD

GREAT LAD CRAG

YEWBARROW 2058ft (628m)

N

W — E

S

ROUGH CRAG

OVERBECK BRIDGE CAR PARK

START

TO WASDALE HEAD

WAST WATER

TO WASDALE HALL

ROUTE SUMMARY

MAP:	OS Outdoor Leisure Map 6
START:	Overbeck Bridge car park, Wasdale, GR 168068
DISTANCE:	Approximately 7½ miles
TIME:	4 – 4½ hours
DIFFICULTY:	High-level route, steep climbs and descents, two scrambles

SCOAT TARN

CHAPTER 16

TORVER, LONG MOSS AND KELLY HALL TARNS

A bright September day at Torver Tarn. Looking north from near the dam
Right: An autumn afternoon on Coniston Water's western shore

Situated to the west of Coniston Water, the parish of Torver consists of three areas known as High Common, Low Common and Back Common. Their boundaries reach from the craggy heights of Dow Crag, Brown Pike and White Maiden down to Coniston's shore, with these peaks and Coniston Old Man dominating the whole region.

A sheltered valley lies where the three commons come together, and it is here, in rich arable land, that the A593 and A5084 meet at Torver village. For most travellers, this tiny settlement is merely a point along the way to Coniston village in the north or to the southern lowlands, and few become acquainted with the variety of walks available around it.

From Torver village, the A5084 branches eastwards to Coniston Water. Approximately ¾ mile (1km) along the road at Beckstones, there is a large parking area opposite a Land Rover dealership. This provides the base for a very comfortable low-level walk of slightly under 4 miles (6.5km). Two hours is ample time to cover the route, which incorporates three tarns and a lengthy passage along the lake shore.

THE WALK

The first few yards follow the road, with the high skyline around Coniston Old Man looming large. From these peaks the land falls through High Common's moorland towards the valley. Very soon, a track drops down into the valley basin and passes over Torver Beck by way of an old stone bridge. The surroundings here are of fields and trees, the distant mountains passing out of view for the moment. Then the outlook changes quickly to bracken and open moorland as our route rises gently towards Torver Tarn. The mountains reappear as the path approaches and then skirts around a hill know as Anne Rigg, where the tarn is revealed ahead.

Torver Tarn lies in a hollow between rocky outcrops, at an altitude of 374ft (114m). Today the surroundings are of open moorland, the result of total deforestation from the sixteenth century onwards, when a plethora of iron bloomeries exploited the woodland for fuel. The remains of the bloomeries and their attendant spoil heaps are dotted around the whole Torver area, although nature has largely mellowed their outlines to conform with the general landscape. The land slopes gently on the south-eastern side up to outcrops on Torver Low Common. On both the eastern and the western sides, the land is again gently sloping, while the northern tip is very flat and open. It is this northern aspect that offers the finest views, passing on from the Coniston Fells over central Lakeland to the peaks beyond Grasmere.

From the tarn to the Coniston Fells, the land rises over High Common, an area rich in stone circles, cairns and ancient earthworks. Settlers during the Bronze Age were the first to cut small clearings in the forest, where they built burial cairns and meeting places. Further open patches were made by the first iron smelters. A number of very small unnamed tarns can be found in the undulating ground over to the west, before the outcrops fall down to the main Torver valley. The wide open aspect of Torver Tarn gives it a very bright, cheerful atmosphere that requires practically no effort at all to enjoy, as it lies only twenty minutes from the starting point of our journey.

The tarn measures about 100yd (30m) from east to west, and about 420yd (130m) from north to south, with welcoming, grassy banks. A small headland divides the southern end into two distinct forks, with a very shallow western fork and a smaller, deeper eastern one which terminates at a small dam. This dam was constructed to increase the water supply to a mill down at Sunny Bank, the last surviving major industry in the area. The eastern shore offers the firmest access points to this very attractive water, which is fed by an inlet stream that comes down from the higher ground of Green How and Grey Stone, entering by the marshy south-western corner.

On leaving the tarn, our path enters a narrow valley following its outflow, with the wooded slopes on Coniston's eastern shore forming the horizon. The path is clear and grassy on a gentle descent down to a footbridge over Torver Beck. Here, the beck's tree-lined banks provide shade with dappled sunlight before we rise out of the dell onto the road, crossing directly over it onto a farm track. Moving now towards Coniston Water, the path skirts around an enclosure of small fields known as Delicars. This is believed to have been a shared area in the past, with local farmers taking turns to plant crops in the strips of land.

This section of the route forms one of the loveliest parts of the Cumbria Way, and quickly leads down to the lake. The woods on the opposite shore are completely open to view now, and a narrow strip of trees lines both our path and the shingle shoreline. A wooden bench marks the beginning of the waterside pathway, placed there by a Mr and Mrs Sumner in memory of their son. Before his loss, and prior to changes in the rules governing land use, successive generations of the Sumner family camped here every summer for sixty consecutive years. Tracks made by them can still be discerned in the ground, despite ever-increasing coverage by bracken. Even when the tracks have finally disappeared, the memory of the Sumners' visits will still remain both in the bench and in the tree closest to it, which they planted during the Second World War.

It is possible to walk along the shore itself for much of this section. If you choose to do this, make sure to rejoin the path where a fence crosses your way. Soon after this the path heads away from the shoreline and climbs up through the woods.

Although Coniston Water presents a very peaceful scene, with fewer surface craft than one might expect, it is well known as the

Right: Long Moss Tarn in October sunshine.
Looking east towards Coniston Water

lake where Sir Donald Campbell raced his record-breaking boat *Bluebird*. In 1967 he was the holder of both land and water speed records, but was not content with the water speed of 276.3mph (442kph). In January he attempted to better it, and succeeded on his first run, achieving a speed of slightly over 300mph (480kph). However, it was the second run that is particularly remembered; the boat performed that infamous backward somersault, and Sir Donald Campbell was lost forever.

For those who continue along the path, the narrow band of trees expands up and away from the lake, heading to the top of Torver Back Common on the left. That is where the remaining tarns of the day lie. The path crosses Moor Gill at a point where an iron bloomery used to stand, then enters the deepest part of Torver Common Wood. Soon it bends sharply to the left and climbs up through trees into open land and the common. Red squirrels are usually in evidence

over the final section of woodland and considering their timid nature, those hereabouts seem surprisingly undaunted by human passers-by. The way now passes over undulating ground covered in bracken and grass, broken by various rocky outcrops before arriving at Long Moss Tarn.

'Long Moss' is an apt description of this tarn. It consists mainly of very shallow water, reeds and marshes, about 200yd (180m) in length and 30yd (27m) across. However, the setting is impressive, with open moorland on three sides and the highest point of the common's ridge on the other. Looking towards the outflow from the ridge reveals Coniston Water and its far woods, which form part of the great Grizedale Forest. Beyond this, a dark and distant horizon is formed by the eastern fells, which provide a contrast to the softer, rolling aspect of the tarn's immediate surroundings. The water does not reach a sufficient depth for swimming at any point, but one can still cool off aching feet or heated brows by the water's edge.

The end of the journey is only a few minutes away, but before we reach the car park the path skirts a delightful little water known as Kelly Hall Tarn. Once again, the Coniston Fells form a backdrop to the north-western outlook beyond High Common. Closer to the tarn, woodland on the opposite side of the valley gives way to rich arable land which leads up to a gentle slope, where the tarn rests in a shallow hollow. A few trees are reflected on the shining surface, surrounded by grassy banks and bracken which glows bright gold in the autumn, adding to a very colourful scene. The tarn is roughly circular in shape, with a diameter of perhaps 50yd (15m). The clean water was used until very recently as a private drinking supply, and was drawn through a tap built into the small dam at the outflow. The road and car park are just a matter of a few yards away, and many people come to picnic by the grassy shoreline. It represents an ideal ending to a very enjoyable and easy route for all categories of walkers.

Above: Autumn colours at Kelly Hall Tarn, looking towards Torver High Common

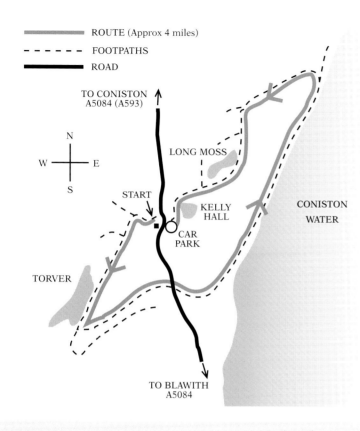

Legend

- ROUTE (Approx 4 miles)
- FOOTPATHS
- ROAD

TO CONISTON
A5084 (A593)

N
W — E
S

LONG MOSS

START

KELLY
HALL

CONISTON
WATER

CAR
PARK

TORVER

TO BLAWITH
A5084

ROUTE SUMMARY

MAP: OS Outdoor Leisure Map 6

START: Car park at Beckstones, GR 287931

DISTANCE: Approximately 4 miles (6.5km)

TIME: 2 – 2½ hours

DIFFICULTY: None

ROUTE DIRECTIONS

The car park is on the A5084, opposite a Land Rover dealership at Beckstones.

1 From there, turn right along the road and then left on the track that leads down between a wall and a line of trees. A wooden sign marked 'Bridleway' shows the way.

2 The track comes to a gate, after which it forks. Take the right branch over the bridge and then turn left following a blue direction indicator.

3 This leads to another gate and then almost immediately to another fork in the path. The right branch is the more obvious one, but our way is to the left over a faint, grassy track.

4 This follows a wall on the left, and then curves away from the wall before arriving at a cross-path. Carry straight on here, and at the top of a small rise, Torver Tarn can be seen ahead.

5 Carry on along the tarn's eastern shore to the dam, and then a further 20yd (18m) or so to another cross-path.

6 Cut straight across and follow the path into a valley where the tarn's outflow stream flows down on your right. Make sure that you are on this path, not the far one where the stream would be on your left. If you follow that one, you will have to walk up the main road later to regain the correct route.

7 The path comes down to a footbridge over Torver Beck and then turns right and up to the road.

8 Cross over the road to the farm track signposted 'Public Footpath Coniston via Lake Shore'.

9 Follow the track down towards the lake. After passing through a gate, ignore any branches that you see going to the left and stay on the main path to the lake shore.

10 From here the path is clear and unbroken along the shoreline. Cross over a beck and carry on to a gate.

11 Soon after this, the path bends sharply to the left where another branches to the right, continuing close to the shore. Take the path to the left and upwards through the woods.

12 At a stile, the path becomes unclear. Continue in the same general direction, but bear slightly to the right where once again the path becomes obvious.

13 Soon you leave the tree line and enter a clearing. A wide, grassy path carries on through bracken and then arrives at another large clearing.

14 On the far side of the clearing a high knoll stands directly ahead of you. Skirt to the right (west) of it to pick up the path.

15 Around this area the paths on the ground differ considerably from those on Ordnance Survey maps, and the route passes by Long Moss Tarn to the south-east, not north-west as marked on the O.S. map.

16 Where the path forks after leaving the tarn, bear right and follow the wall-side path down to Kelly Hall Tarn.

17 Continue along the same path from there to a gate at the rear of the car park.

CHAPTER 17

BEACON TARN

The tranquil surface of Beacon Tarn reflects the fading colours of an autumn evening

The Blawith Fells and Beacon Tarn lie to the south of Torver, with the tarn adjacent to Coniston Water's southernmost reaches. Like the Torver area, the undulating ground of the Blawith Fells has an association with ancient peoples and various cairns and ruins can be found in the vicinity. There is a comfortable walk from the lake shore across the fells, visiting Beacon Tarn. It is the most southerly of our routes, and is slightly under 4 miles (6.5km) long. There are no tiring climbs or very steep descents along the way, and two hours is more than enough to complete it.

THE WALK

From a lake-shore picnic area near Brown Howe, the route follows a lane that marks the boundary between a National Park access area and private land. This first leg of the journey is a very pleasant stroll through woods and farmland, twisting one way and then the other until we reach the point where we leave the lane and head off into fells and moorland. The path skirts the lower slopes of the Blawith Fells, with the vast moorland of Torver Low Common to the north. Beyond the common, the Coniston and Furness Fells form a long, jagged horizon, and Torver Tarn enters the picture as the path begins to climb through a bracken-covered gully. This part of our route follows a section of the Cumbria Way.

As we climb higher, a look backwards shows the V-shape of the dry gully, through which Coniston Old Man dominates the skyline. After passing over the first rise, an area of marsh and grasses lies between the parts of Blawith Fells known as Beacon and Fisher High. It looks as though a tarn should occupy the space, and I am sure that if there were any moraine at the top of the gully, there would indeed be a charming little water here. However, as it stands now, it looks just like a tarn of grass.

As one would expect from the name, the high ground of Beacon to our left was once the site of a signal fire. It is too low to have been part of the national network, and was probably used for local contingencies. The path skirts around Beacon to reveal the tarn ahead and below, at an altitude of 530ft (162m). It presents a very attractive picture, nestled in a hollow between bracken-covered slopes that are coloured here and there with splashes of heather. On our approach, the high land immediately to the south of the tarn is formed by Wool Knott, while to the west the gradient is gentler, offering views of sunsets throughout the year. From the southern end, the view to the north shows the Coniston Fells rising above the tarn's immediate surroundings, while to the south lie the lowlands and part of Morecambe Bay.

Beacon Tarn is a large water, about 500yd (460m) from north to south and 170yd (160m) at the widest point. The maximum depth is about 25ft (8m), with the deepest water close to the eastern shore. It holds many brown trout and perch, and I have heard rumours that there might be a few char. The tarn used to have a great reputation as a pike water, but I am told by Mr Sumner, who was mentioned in Chapter 16, that they were taken out during the war to supplement rations. Nobody seems to be certain if any survived.

A path runs along the rocky, steep eastern shore, forming a narrow ledge in some places where the rock outcrops plunge down to the water. Apart from these sections, the shore is most accessible on this side, near the deep water. The western side appears to be grassy and dry, but there are a few marshy patches there. Inlet streams come in from the west, north and east, and the outflow escapes from the southern tip and then flows to the east, bound for the River Crake.

Although the tarn looks at its best in broad daylight during summer and early autumn, when the heather provides some contrast to

the dominant bracken, at other times of year a good sunset can set the surroundings aglow, brightly illuminating the golden brown ferns and grasses. Far over to the west, Black Combe, Thwaites and Corney Fells block the last rays before the sun dips into the sea, but the view of its setting is memorable nevertheless.

Our path follows the outflow from the tarn, and descends into an area of undulating knolls and outcrops covered in ferns. Here, the far peaks disappear from view until we climb to Slatestone Fell. The wooded eastern shores of Coniston Water appear first, and then the full length of the lake is revealed, with a background of distant peaks forming the northern horizon. Nearing the end of the day, the sails

Above: Beacon Tarn shimmers under a bright autumn sky

of the boats harboured around the lake's quiet southern reaches are picked out by the sun's low rays. Long shadows fill the small hollows around us, with the numerous small outcrops and pinnacles ablaze with light.

Soon the path drops down from the fell and reaches the road.

A few yards north of here, a number of paths lead down to the lake shore from a car park. Unfortunately, they all seem to enter private ground so it is necessary to complete the last $^1/_2$ mile (1km) on tarmac. But even this is a pleasant section, shaded by trees along much of the way.

Above: Coniston Water in the last sunshine of an October day.
Viewed from the route near Beacon Tarn

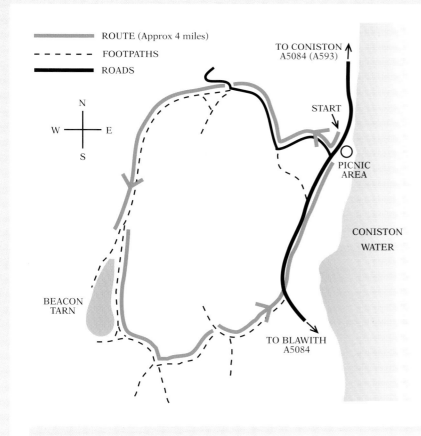

ROUTE (Approx 4 miles)	
FOOTPATHS	
ROADS	

N
W — E
S

TO CONISTON
A5084 (A593)

START

PICNIC
AREA

CONISTON
WATER

BEACON
TARN

TO BLAWITH
A5084

ROUTE SUMMARY

MAP: OS Landranger Map 96

START: Picnic area near Brown Howe, GR 290911

DISTANCE: Approximately 4 miles (6.5km)

TIME: 2 hours

DIFFICULTY: None

ROUTE DIRECTIONS

The picnic area which marks the start of the walk can be found on the lake shore near Brown Howe, about 1½ miles (2.5km) south of Beckstones on the A5084.

1 From there, turn left along the road for about 100yd (90m), and then right along a lane. At the beginning of the lane you will see a National Park sign introducing Blawith Common.

2 Where the lane curves sharply to the right, a wooden 'Public Footpath' sign points to the left. Go past this and continue along the lane.

3 At the next sharp bend to the right, you will see a grass track branching off to the left (west). Take this track, and after about 200yd (180m) take the right branch (in effect straight on) where the track forks.

4 Soon after this, the track arrives at a large clump of reeds and tall grasses. Skirt to the left of this. Ordnance Survey maps show another path that branches sharply to the left along this section, but it is not obvious on the ground. If you happen to see it carry on past it.

5 Where another, quite distinct fork appears, bear left, heading slightly up the high ground on your left. If you are in any doubt on this section, your general direction should aim for the gully between the hillsides, which lies ahead and slightly to your left.

6 Once in the gully, the path heads south, and remains obvious all the way to Beacon Tarn.

7 At the tarn, it splits into two. One branch follows close by the eastern shore and the other, which is easier, continues on higher ground. You can take either as far as the outflow beck at the tarn's southern tip.

8 From there, cross the beck and follow a grassy track to the east, with the beck on your left. Another path joins from the left as you descend to a small footbridge.

9 Turn left (north-east) immediately after the footbridge, climbing up the hillside towards Slatestone Fell.

10 The path then drops down steeply towards another path which cuts across it. Turn right at the T, and head down to the road. If you see any branches to the right between the T and the road, ignore them, and stay on the main path.

11 Turn left on the road to return to the picnic area.

BEACON TARN

CHAPTER 18

MOSS ECCLES AND WISE EEN TARNS

The garden and farmhouse at Hill Top, former residence of Beatrix Potter

On Windermere's western shore, near Belle Isle, stands a broad, densely forested ridge known as Claife Heights. Reaching from Low Wray in the north to High Cunsey in the south, it descends westwards to Esthwaite Water. After the lake, the land rises up to the great Satterthwaite and Grizedale Forests. A cluster of tarns have been formed on the undulating ground of Claife, partly by nature but mainly by the damming of the wetlands in the hollows. The two largest, Moss Eccles and Wise Een are visited on this walk.

Assuming that you do not arrive via the Windermere Ferry, it is certain that your road will have passed through the pastoral setting around Esthwaite water with its magnificent views of the Coniston and Central Fells. The old-world charm of Hawkshead village, where Wordsworth attended grammar school, lies just beyond the northern tip of the lake.

Overlooking these waters, close by the south-western shore, an idyllic collection of farmhouses and cottages constitute the hamlet of Near Sawrey. This is the base for a ramble through woods and tarns that can be enjoyed by young or old, experienced walkers or absolute beginners.

There is a large, free car park on the edge of the hamlet for customers of the Tower Bank Arms and the National Trust property next to it. On leaving your vehicle, you might think that you have travelled much further than you intended as you gaze upon a sea of oriental faces. The National Trust property is the reason. Named Hill Top Farm, it was the first Lakeland purchase of Beatrix Potter, and is now a shrine for her admirers – one in five of them travelling from Japan. As they usually arrive by the coachload, the effect can be wonderfully chaotic.

The Lake District provides the setting for most of Beatrix Potter's animal stories, but she was already a successful author before she discovered Sawrey in 1896, her thirtieth year. It was a further

154

nine years before she finalised the purchase of the seventeenth century farmhouse Hill Top, financing the transaction mainly through sales of *The Tale of Peter Rabbit*. Her arrival here marked the start of her busiest years. With the exception of *The Tale of Johnny Town Mouse*, which was set in the narrow, cobbled streets and alleyways of Hawkshead, everything she wrote after 1905 was set in or around Near Sawrey.

She must have possessed boundless energy, for in addition to her prodigious output of children's books she also worked long hours on the farm and accumulated numerous other properties. Her main acquisition was the Monk Coniston Estate. For seven years she managed the estate herself, collecting rents, supervising repairs and taking an active part in all areas of the work. Half of the estate was then sold to the National Trust without taking any profit.

She also found time to help in the upkeep of other farms and cottages throughout the Lakes regardless of their ownership, paying particular attention to conservation issues. But the work closest to her heart involved the propagation of the native Herdwick sheep. This is a very hardy breed, particularly suited for life on the fells. It has hard-wearing, water-resistant wool and is an instinctive survivor, knowing which areas to avoid during bad weather. Strongly territorial, Herdwicks will often return to their individual patch on the hills after the winter's snows. Nowadays they are easily the dominant local breed.

On Beatrix Potter's death in 1943, over 4,000 acres (1,600ha) of prime Lakeland landscape were bequeathed to the National Trust, with the instruction that everything in Hill Top 'should be left in their present condition'. The house is now a honeypot for enthusiasts, with the original furniture and countless artifacts and sketches. It is open from Saturdays to Wednesdays, between April and October.

Beatrix Potter's ashes were scattered somewhere in the area by

Early summer at Moss Eccles Tarn

her trusted farm bailiff, but the exact location was kept so secret that not even her husband knew it.

In keeping with the Potter landscapes, our route initially passes through classic English countryside of gently rolling fields, with grassy knolls and woodland. Rising gradually on farm tracks, the first destination is Moss Eccles Tarn, located above Near Sawrey at 550ft (168m). A U-shaped water, it measures around 300yd by 200yd (275m by 180m). Wide open on the eastern shore where the track passes, it becomes tree-lined towards the western tip. The deepest water is found at the dam, around which most anglers try their luck. A National Trust property, it is stocked annually with brown trout. Fishing permits (fly fishing only) are available from the Tower Bank Arms. For those wishing to explore further, a path crosses the dam and goes on into the wooded section of the shore.

On leaving the tarn, the landscape opens out behind us on the approach to a hill crest, revealing the southern reaches of Windermere. At the top of the rise, Wise Een Tarn is seen ahead at an altitude of 750ft (229m). This is a larger water, around 450yd (410m) long and 220yd (200m) at its widest point. Forested behind the western shore, the ground opens at the dam on the north-western edge near a boat-house. After this the land falls away to present a wonderful panorama that includes all the fells around the Langdales. On fine summer evenings the sun arcs down and sets beyond the distant peaks, casting low rays straight across the water. This is certainly the most accessible spot in the Lake District where such a spectacle can be seen. Even in dull weather this view has a timeless quality, guaranteed to capture everyone's attention.

Wise Een is privately owned. It was once used for research by the Freshwater Biological Institute. No fishing is allowed, partly to protect the wildlife in the marshland that encroaches onto the shore and the swans that are usually in evidence on the tarn's placid, shining

Windermere, with Belle Isle and Bowness viewed from Claife Heights

surface. The track now heads up to the woods on Claife Heights. Instantly the air becomes cooler amongst the trees, and is heavily spiced with the fresh tang of pine. A thick carpet of pine needles lies underfoot in the more densely forested sections. Then the ground clears at the first viewpoint, from where Ambleside and its backdrop of mountains are clearly visible.

The next viewpoint comes at High Blind How where all of southern Windermere, Bowness and Windermere village are seen to the east. To the north-west the Langdale Peaks are evident once more, and it seems as though there cannot be a better vista within these woods – a false impression.

Having threaded through more deep, dark forest, the path arrives on a headland above central Windermere, looking down on Belle Isle and its satellite islands. On the far shore are the massed jetties and marinas of Bowness town, which spreads up to merge with Windermere village. Together they form the largest tourist centre in the Lake District and many visitors venture no further into Lakeland than this.

Windermere has always been the main commercial centre of the region because of its railhead, but in the 1960s, the new Kendal bypass and the M6 brought it within easy reach of the massive populations of the northern cities – currently, 14 million people visit it every year. The boom years of the 1960s and 1970s brought a swift increase in private moorings on the lake. Now, on warm weekends, the waterways of the central islands swarm with yachts and power-boats, the drone of the lake traffic providing a stark contrast to the birdsong and gentle rustling of trees up here on our viewpoint. The shore lies just 550ft (170m) below, but feels like a whole world away.

Long ago, the sounds coming from the lake could have included the ghostly voice of the Claife Crier. In the days of the rowed ferry from Bowness to Far Sawrey, the Crier is said to have lured passengers and boatmen to their deaths on misty nights. One ferryman who responded to the plaintive call set off across the lake to collect his late passenger, only to return alone and dumb with fright. He died the following day without revealing the cause of his terror. The identity of the voice remains a mystery. Some believe it to be the spectre of one or more of the forty-seven wedding guests who drowned in 1635 when their overladen craft turned turtle. Others maintain that it was the unhappy spirit of the murderer Thomas Lancaster. In 1671 he was hanged at Sawrey Causeway, close to the ferry road. The Crier's antics occurred so regularly that a local priest was obliged to perform an exorcism, committing the spirit to lie entombed in Claife Quarry. All has been quiet since.

Eventually the footpath arrives in Far Sawrey, close to the Sawrey Hotel and its Claife Crier Bar. After this, all that remains is a short stroll along the lane back to Near Sawrey, passing Hill Top on the way.

Although this route covers 5 miles (8km), I recommend it for those seeking to keep their children entertained – they will particularly enjoy the deep woods. Also, with the possible exception of the viewpoint over Belle Isle, where a little stewardship may be called for, this is a very safe walk. Altitude is gained and lost gradually, so no great effort is required.

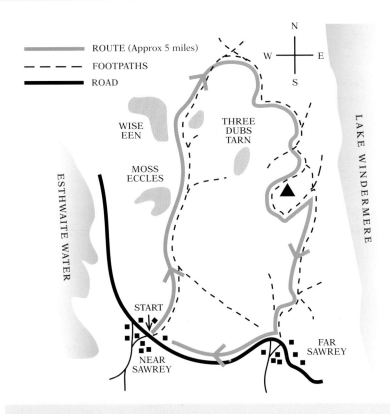

ROUTE (Approx 5 miles)
FOOTPATHS
ROAD

WISE
EEN

THREE
DUBS
TARN

MOSS
ECCLES

ESTHWAITE WATER

LAKE WINDERMERE

START

NEAR
SAWREY

FAR
SAWREY

N
W — E
S

ROUTE SUMMARY

MAP: OS Outdoor Leisure Map 7

START: Near Sawrey, GR 370956

DISTANCE: Approximately 5 miles (8km)

TIME: 2¹/₂ – 3 hours

DIFFICULTY: None

SPECIAL NEEDS: Fishing permit for Moss Eccles Tarn, available
                  from Tower Bank Arms, Near Sawrey

ROUTE DIRECTIONS

1 In Near Sawrey locate the lane opposite the Buckle Peat Guest House. Follow this up through the houses and farm buildings, after which it becomes a track.

2 The first signpost seen points the way to 'Bridleway Claife Heights', which in effect is straight on.

3 After a farm gate, follow the sign 'Claife Heights/The Tarn', and only twenty minutes into the journey, the path arrives at Moss Eccles Tarn.

4 Beyond the tarn the track forks. Bear left here, up to the gate above Wise Een Tarn, after which the track heads up to the tree line.

5 These woods are a maze of paths and tracks, so follow directions carefully. Our route bends to the right soon after entering the trees, and goes down to a signpost.

6 Here the main track curves sharply left, but our way now is to the right on the path through the trees, following the sign 'Footpath Ferry/Far Sawrey'. For a considerable distance after this, the route is marked by white-tipped posts.

7 At the next signpost follow the direction marked 'Footpath Ferry/Far Sawrey'. This takes you to the first viewpoint. The path then drops down to a wider track.

8 Turn right on to this, again following the sign 'Footpath Ferry/Far Sawrey'.

9 A hundred yards (90m) up this track, turn left into the trees, again following the same sign.

10 This path forks as a clearing opens on the right. Take the right fork upwards. A small post at the top of the rise, saying 'Viewpoint', directs you to High Blind How and its triangulation column.

11 Carrying on down, the path comes to a small footbridge where another path crosses the way. Go straight across here, up the wooded slope marked with white-tipped posts.

12 At the top of this rise, a small post points the way to 'Ferry' (look on the opposite side). Then comes another small post with the same legend.

13 Arriving next at a cross-path, you will see a gap in the facing wall. This leads to the best viewpoint of the journey.

14 Come back to the wall and turn left, following the sign 'Footpath Far Sawrey'.

15 After a farm gate and stile, a path is seen branching to the right. Ignore this and follow the track signposted 'Ferry'. You soon reach a major cross-track. Follow the sign marked 'Bridleway Far Sawrey', turning right and through the farm gate.

16 At Far Sawrey turn right on to the lane to return to Near Sawrey.

INDEX

INDEX